GOD'S

GUIDANCE

SYSTEM

SETTING YOUR COURSE FOR DESTINY

BY
LES BROWN

God's Guidance System
Copyright © 1998 by Dr. Leslie Brown

McDougal Publishing is a ministry of The McDougal Foundation, Inc., a Maryland nonprofit corporation dedicated to spreading the Gospel of the Lord Jesus Christ to as many people as possible in the shortest time possible.

Published by:

McDougal Publishing
P.O. Box 3595
Hagerstown, MD 21742-3595

ISBN 1-884369-95-2

Printed in the United States of America
For Worldwide Distribution

DEDICATION

I would like to dedicate this book to my dad, James M. Brown, a recent resident of Heaven. In his eighty years on this Earth, his love, simple values and hard work were an inspiration to my life. He was short on education but long on wisdom and common sense.

He "played hurt" the last twelve years of life's game, his body wracked with pain and infirmity. He didn't quit or ask the Heavenly Coach to "bench him" until he was assured that he had fulfilled his purpose. Then, with gentle grace, he left the game so that someone else could play.

Dad, your voice will be greatly missed.

For as many as are led by the Spirit of God, these are sons of God.

Romans 8:14

Contents

Foreword by Judson Cornwall 7

Introduction 9

Part I: Understanding God's Guidance System 11

1. Principles of Guidance 13

2. Hindrances to Guidance 25

Part II: The Seven Biblical Principles of

   Guidance 41

3. The Inner Conviction of the Spirit 43

4. The Scriptures 61

5. Prophecy 79

6. Godly Counsel 101

7. Circumstances 121

8. The Peace of God 147

9. The Provision of God 171

Part III: The Application... 195

10. Applying These Truths to YOUR Life 197

Foreword
by Judson Cornwall

"Show me the way!" is today's popular cry. Many of our current bestselling books are "How to ..." books. Guidance! That's the need of the hour. Every new product spawns a myriad of instructions and magazines to show us how to use it best. Personal counseling is on the upswing. Psychiatrists are in great demand. Psychic guides advertise on television and fill the Internet. Even world leaders have surrounded themselves with guidance counselors.

It is not that we are ignorant. Americans have access to more information than ever before. We just don't know how to use that information. We are like a boat in a dense fog. Somehow we have forgotten where the guidance buoys and harbor lights are to be found. Having exchanged the counsel of God's Word for the wisdom of men, we've lost our perspective. We have great motion, but we don't know where we are going or how to get there.

Unfortunately, this same situation seems to apply to many Christians. In the multitude of voices calling to them and declaring, "This is the way," they have become confused and disoriented. Is it conceivable that God would lead us out of sin into salvation without providing guidance for living the Christian life? No! Jesus clearly stated, *"My sheep listen to my voice; I know them, and they follow me"* (John 10:27, NIV). Whether or not this seems to be consistently occurring in the lives of Christians we observe in today's society, it is a clear provision of Jesus for all His followers. He knows the way; we need but follow Him. If we are confused, it is because we have failed to follow *God's Guidance System.*

Dr. Leslie Brown has faced this problem in his personal life, in the lives of many parishioners he has pastored, and in his counseling of people outside his church. I have known Dr. Brown for more than twenty years and have ministered in his church and with him outside his church. The lessons he teaches in this book come less from theory and more from hard knocks and much observation. He does not write so much as a learned theologian, but as a concerned pastor. He has rescued many wandering Christians with these simple principles. He has also watched Christians ignore these principles and make a shipwreck of their lives on the rocks of adversity.

God's guidance for individual lives is available and very practical. There is nothing mystical in the teachings in this book. It is practical, personal, and practiced, and I highly recommend it to every believer.

INTRODUCTION

One of my first jobs after I moved here to the famed island of Maui was chartering a fishing boat out of the harbor. I was first mate on that boat for about a year. Occasionally we would go out during the day and be out so long that we had to come back in the dark. When visibility was thus limited, the captain didn't just aim for the harbor and go full speed ahead. He knew that if he did that he would probably hit a reef and founder. We had a deep-hulled boat that had to come safely into a shallow-water harbor, and the boat and the people it carried were valuable enough that this could not be left to chance.

To reach the harbor safely, the captain had to line the boat up according to the buoy lights that were placed in the water to guide boats like ours safely in. He could not be guided by any single marker. There were a whole series of markers, and he had to line the boat up between them all to assure that we were taking a safe course that would bring the boat safely into port.

This system was developed over time because of the sad experiences of captains who were not successful in bringing their boats safely into port and had suffered great loss of property and life. Piloting a boat is serious business, and we were blessed with the establishment of a safe system of guidance for those who were willing to follow it.

God has placed shining buoy lights in the sea of your life, and if you intend to pilot your boat safely into life's harbor, you must line up according to those lights. You must learn to recognize the buoys He has placed, learning to know them well enough that you can easily and quickly bring yourself into line with them. If you fail to do this, you may quickly find yourself shipwrecked along the shoals.

Each of us was encoded at birth with a unique and specialized purpose and destiny. No one else can do what you were born to do, and no one else can do what I was born to do. The problem begins, for many of us, when we begin to feel that our dreams and God's will are incompatible, that God's will could very well be unattainable and that, should we be able to attain it, we might not find any joy in the fulfillment. We fail to realize that our dreams are, for the most part, dreams that God has given us to pursue and attain, and knowing His will and being guided by His Spirit can help us achieve all our dreams in life.

We desperately need guidance, not only to plot our course, but to maintain that course as we navigate through life. This is a matter of life and death, a question of prosperity or great loss, a matter of health or tragic sickness. Finding God's course for our lives will result in untold blessing here in this life and an entrance into life eternal, while missing His course may mean sudden destruction for us and all those aboard our ship. Nothing could be more important!

My desire is that this book will help you discover or rediscover *God's Guidance System* which is able to bring you safely and victoriously to your eternal destination.

Les Brown
Maui, Hawaii

Part I:

Understanding
God's Guidance System

CHAPTER 1

PRINCIPLES OF GUIDANCE

For as many as are led by the Spirit of God, these are sons of God. Romans 8:14

Who or what is leading you? It sounds like a simple question, doesn't it? But it's crucial to success in this Christian life. If you want to be called a son of God, then you must be led by His Spirit.

Many people today are looking for supernatural guidance of one kind or another. Millions are calling psychic hotlines, while the older businesses of palm reading, horoscopes and divination are still booming in what is supposed to be a more enlightened age. As Christians, we understand that these are not for us. Our leading, our guidance, must come from the Lord. Our hearts cry out for Him to lead us and to teach us His ways.

But how do we know that we have heard His response to us? How are we to discern whether we are truly being led of the Lord?

Nothing is more important to the Christian than the guidance that he gets and, according to the Scriptures,

13

we are to be led by the Spirit of God, not by the spirit of man, the spirit of the age or the will of flesh. Many of us have a lot of room to grow in this area.

An Example of Wrong Guidance

The story is told of a businessman who was a new Christian and didn't know a lot about guidance or about how to get direction from the Lord. He was wondering what to do with his company and his investments, so he decided to go to the Word of God for an answer. He prayed, "God, I'm going to open my Bible and put my finger down on a page. Whatever my finger lands on, I'm going to take as a word from You." He did this, and his finger pointed to the word "wheat." He took that as a word from the Lord that he should put all of his investments into the wheat market. He did so, and the result was that he made a fortune.

Because he had been successful the first time, he didn't mature in his method of being guided and after a time thought, *This market can't last forever*, so he decided to go to the Word of God again concerning what he should do with the profits he was making. He opened the Bible, put his finger down, and this time his finger was pointing to the word "oil." He took all of his funds out of wheat and invested in oil, and, again he made a fortune.

When the market got a little shaky, the man briefly considered selling his oil investments, but he reasoned, *Oil is something that everybody must have, so I'll just hang in there and surely I'll come out okay in the long run*. The bottom fell out of oil, however, and he lost most of his money.

Principles of Guidance

Now the man didn't know what to do next. He was in jeopardy of losing even more, so he went back to the Bible. This time his finger landed on the words "Chapter Eleven," and he decided that God wanted him to file for bankruptcy.

Believe it or not, this is the way many believers approach guidance. Guidance from God, however, is not something to play with or to assume. We cannot afford to gamble with our futures. It is important that we learn to rely on God's indications alone. Failure to receive or to heed His direction can bring about His judgment on our lives.

When the Israelites under Moses failed to heed the direction and guidance of God, He judged them. He simply stopped guiding them, and they wandered about for the next forty years until most of them died in the wilderness.

The Israelites in the wilderness had motion, but they had no direction, and many Christians today are just like that. This is why we so desperately need *God's Guidance System* at work in our lives.

We cannot trust our own instincts. The Scriptures declare:

> *There is a way that seems right to a man,*
> *But its end is the way of death.*   Proverbs 14:12

Our ways are not God's ways. God does not want us to wander aimlessly, and He also does not want us to have to constantly question whether or not we are hearing from Him. Our God is not the author of confusion. He wants us to become mature people who can govern our own lives, who can make appropriate and wise decisions and who will not be *"tossed to and fro ... with every wind of doctrine"* (Ephesians 4:14). We don't have to be mature to get to Heaven, but we do have to be mature in order to succeed in this life. If your life is shrouded in indecision, there is good news. God wants you to have clear direction and has provided the means of supplying it.

God's direction of the Hebrews in the Old Testament book of Exodus was easy to discern. He guided them through the wilderness with a cloud by day and a pillar of fire by night. He told them, "When the cloud moves, you move, and when the cloud remains, you remain." That seems like it would be hard to miss, doesn't it? Yet there were people who missed it, and we will learn the reasons they missed it.

Things changed in the New Testament. Today God's guidance system is within the believer. We have no clouds or pillars of fire, because God's guidance is now internal rather than external. It is spiritual, not natural. It is safe, yet many also miss it.

The Danger of Human Rationale

As we begin our look at *God's Guidance System*, we must understand that there are two extremes which will lead us into error if we are not careful. The first is human rationale, and the second is mysticism.

Human rationale never moves out of the realm of what is seen, what is known or what appears to be logical to the human mind. This mentality says, "After all questions have been answered, all doors have been opened, all risk has been eliminated, then we will go forth in faith." But there's not much faith in that!

This extreme is exactly opposite of the biblical command to *"walk by faith, not by sight"* (2 Corinthians 5:7). If we walk by faith, there will be some risks. The human mind always counts it a risk when we step out into the unknown, trusting in God to hold us up, when, in reality, the risk is in not trusting Him.

People walking in the realm of human logic tend to ignore the inner conviction of the Spirit and the peace of God. They also tend to try to overbalance the prophetic word with intellectual reasoning.

A good example of human rationale is found in the story of Paul appearing before King Agrippa. When Paul was being held captive, he had the opportunity to speak with the king (who was trying to help set forth the charges against God's servant). Paul was able to preach to the king, and the king listened intently to him. Agrippa had studied the things of which Paul spoke, but he had learned with his intellect, not with his spirit. His response to Paul's teaching reflects this: *"You almost persuade me to become a Christian"* (Acts 26:28).

Why was Agrippa not fully convinced? It was because he was looking at the things of which Paul spoke with his intellect and his logic. He could not lay these aside long enough to take the necessary leap of faith.

The Danger of Mysticism

The second extreme we must be aware of is mysticism. Some people are led by the unseeable, the unknowable, the uncertain. Those who allow this extreme to govern their lives sometimes say, "I feel led." Whenever such a person wants an excuse for doing whatever it is that they want to do, they may repeat: "I feel led." That may sound spiritual, but if it is not backed up with specific leading from God, it becomes dangerous, a recipe for disaster. Such people move in the subjective realm, ignoring the Scriptures, ignoring wise counsel and ignoring other basic means by which we Christians gain our direction, and they find themselves, consequently, in one crisis after another.

The biblical story of Naaman shows us the dangers of mysticism. Naaman was a captain in the Syrian army. He was also afflicted with leprosy. Along with this curse, however, came a blessing: his wife's young servant girl, an Israelite, gave faithful testimony of what the Lord could do and directed him to Elisha the prophet. Naaman, therefore, went to Israel to be healed. The prophet failed to meet his expectations:

> *Then Naaman went with his horses and chariot, and he stood at the door of Elisha's house. And Elisha sent a messenger to him, saying, "Go and wash in the Jordan seven times, and your flesh shall be restored to you, and you shall be clean." But Naaman became furious, and went away and said, "Indeed, I said to myself, 'He will surely come out to me, and stand and call on the name of the LORD his God, and wave his hand over the place, and heal the leprosy.' Are not the Abanah and the Pharpar, the rivers of Damascus, better than all the waters of Israel? Could I not wash in them and be clean?" So he turned and went away in a rage.* 2 Kings 5:9-12

Principles of Guidance

Naaman had come to the prophet, carrying with him a load of expectations. He wanted God to do things his way. He thought he knew just how God would behave, and he was looking for the externals — the waving of the hand, the prophetic pronouncement. He wasn't expecting anything so simple as a bath in the river.

Many Christians today are just like Naaman. They go from place to place looking for the externals which meet their expectations of God at work. What was Naaman really saying? By his actions he was declaring, "If the prophet doesn't do all this, then it can't be genuine healing." Fortunately for him, he listened to the advice of his servants, obeyed the word of the Lord and walked away from the Jordan healed of his leprosy.

Some modern believers say, "If I am not slain in the Spirit, then I cannot be healed." "If I don't see fireworks or the Shekinah glory, I can't be healed." "Yes, someone laid their hands on me and prayed, but I didn't feel anything. There must be more to it than that, or I will not be healed." And when they go home — surprise, surprise — they are not healed. Why? Their expectations keep them from receiving the miracle God has for them.

We cannot operate in mysticism. I have nothing against being slain in the Spirit or against holy laughter or other manifestations of the Holy Spirit. These things take place continually in the church that God has called me to pastor. But we cannot look to these things for guidance because the Lord does not always operate in the same way, and because there is too much room for us to operate in our emotions when we depend on outward manifestations.

God's Guidance System

So what are we to do? We must be led by the Spirit of God, not by our emotions or our logic and knowledge. We must be aware of the means He has chosen to use in leading His people.

TOO MANY VOICES

One of the first things we need to do when we seek the guidance of the Lord is to get into a position where we are free to hear Him and to distinguish His voice. There are many voices vying for our attention. Paul wrote:

There are, it may be, so many kinds of languages in the world, and none of them is without significance.
1 Corinthians 14:10

Because we are surrounded by so many voices, we must decide which of them we truly want to hear. If we want to hear from God, we must sometimes turn off the television or put down the newspapers and magazines or turn off the stereo and even sometimes take the phone off the hook. Not all the voices clamoring for our attention are wise, so we must be careful who we hear.

I'm not saying that these mediums of communication are all bad. God has many ways of bringing His word to us. What I am saying is that if we want to hear from God, we must turn off the competing voices. Part of spiritual maturity is learning to discern God's voice as He speaks to us.

God does speak to us, for He promised through Isaiah:

The LORD will guide you continually.   Isaiah 58:11

20

Principles of Guidance

God is always guiding His people. Our part is to learn to hear Him, to discern His guidance from among the many voices that continually bombard us. We must lay aside our human rationale and our mysticism and come into agreement with His guidance system if we want to walk in the paths He has designed for us.

THE NEED FOR TWO OR THREE WITNESSES

When I worked on that boat in the Maui harbor and saw that by aligning ourselves with the many buoys placed specifically for that purpose we could safely bring our boat and passengers into port, I learned a lesson that has served me well throughout life. If I fail to line up to God's shining buoy lights and disaster comes to my life, I have no one to blame but myself. How can I blame God when He has made every provision for my safety?

I have found that there are seven principles of guidance that God has established to help us. And what are these markers God has placed in the sea of life to guide us safely on our journey? They include inner conviction, the Scriptures, prophetic utterance, godly counsel, circumstances, the peace of God, and the provision of God. These are our buoys — our witnesses — and we will deal with each in more detail in the next section of the book.

Like the buoys at sea, God never guides us by any one witness alone. In making a major decision, therefore, we must never rely on only one of the seven principles. Rather, we should let our answers come with the wisdom of *two or three witnesses.*

The biblical teaching on the subject of two or three

witnesses has sometimes been misunderstood and sometimes taken to extreme. Jesus said:

> *But if he will not hear, take with you one or two more,*
> *that by the mouth of two or three witnesses every word*
> *may be established.*   Matthew 18:16

The Apostle Paul wrote:

> *This will be the third time I am coming to you. "By*
> *the mouth of two or three witnesses every word shall*
> *be established."*   2 Corinthians 13:1

> *Do not receive an accusation against an elder except*
> *from two or three witnesses.*   1 Timothy 5:19

Many of us have been taught that the *"two or three witnesses"* of which the Scriptures speak are two or three different people coming to us and saying the same thing. I believe, however, these two or three witnesses are not people at all but two or three of the seven principles of God's guidance. Two or three of them must be operating in any given situation for us to know that we are being safely guided by God. If we rely on only one buoy, we may become unbalanced or misguided or disoriented and not be able to hear clearly what God is saying.

It could be possible for two people to come to you and say the same thing and both of them be wrong. If they are advising something that is against the clear teaching of the Bible, they obviously are wrong, and their counsel must not be followed. This is a dangerous business. God has some more reliable witnesses that He has placed at our disposal.

Principles of Guidance

Although some have erroneously tried to apply the principles of two or three witnesses to every minute decision of life, we cannot fail to embrace this truth when it comes to the issue of divine guidance. We don't usually need God's guidance in matters concerning what to eat or what to wear, but we certainly do need His input in such major decisions as buying a car or a house, getting married, which college to attend, what career to pursue, and any major business decision. Decisions like these have a great and lasting impact on our own lives and the lives of all those around us. Therefore they must not be taken lightly. We need God's guidance, and we cannot afford to be careless in such matters.

Decisions may take a bit longer to make when we check ourselves by several principles, but that's all right. I, for one, am hesitant to move forward if I do not have the confirmation of two or three witnesses, and I firmly believe that this would be a wise position for every believer to take. God isn't in a hurry, and He knows how to confirm His word to us.

DECISIONS BASED ON PANIC

Too many believers are moved by panic rather than the revealed will of God. They are so desperate for an answer that they grasp at anything as a sign from God. "God, show me a butterfly flying without wings, and I'll believe it's You." This may sound preposterous, but I have heard of many cases just as farfetched as this one.

When we make decisions, we must ask some hard questions based on *God's Guidance System*. If someone calls us on the telephone and gives us a word, we can't afford to get ready to jump off into the unknown with no other spiritual basis than that. We need either a scriptural confirmation, an inner conviction, some godly counsel, some confirming circumstances or an abiding peace from God to show us that what we have been told is truly of the Lord. Trusting God does not mean leaping blindly without any clear indication that He wants us to do it.

The bigger the decision at hand, the more that is at risk, and when this is true, I am in favor of having more witnesses. If we fail to do it, we may find ourselves in some disastrous situation. Although not all situations are irreversible, and God will forgive us and help us when we make mistakes, we could save ourselves a lot of heartache if we could learn to use these seven principles, several at a time.

Most of the errors in our teaching and our understanding of guidance occur, I believe, when any one of these principles is overemphasized to the exclusion of the others. There are many tapes and books available on each of these subjects — personal prophecy, counseling, the peace of God, provision, etc. All of these are good and valid teachings, but we must have a balance of principles at work.

Before we look into each of these principles of guidance in detail, we should first look at some possible hindrances to their effectiveness in our lives.

CHAPTER 2

HINDRANCES TO GUIDANCE

Jesus answered them, "I told you, and you do not believe. The works that I do in My Father's name, they bear witness of Me. But you do not believe, because you are not of My sheep, as I said to you."

John 10:25-26

Although it is easy to hear God's voice and He wants to guide us in this way, it is not guaranteed. There are things that, if we let them, will hinder us from finding God's will for our lives. Let us examine some of them now.

NOT BEING SAVED

The first and most elemental hindrance to finding guidance from God is being lost or unsaved. Jesus declared:

"But he who enters by the door is the shepherd of the sheep. To him the doorkeeper opens, and the sheep hear

his voice; and he calls his own sheep by name and leads them out. And when he brings out his own sheep, he goes before them; and the sheep follow him, for they know his voice. Yet they will by no means follow a stranger, but will flee from him, for they do not know the voice of strangers.

"My sheep hear My voice, and I know them, and they follow Me."   John 10:2-5 and 27

What wonderful reassurance God gives to His Church! So often Christians grow discouraged and say, "I just can't hear from God." Beloved, please don't ever say that again. You *can* hear from God, and anyone who says you cannot is a liar. You have a birthright in God. You are His own, the sheep of His pasture, and God has said, "You know My voice."

Jesus said, *"My sheep hear My voice."* He didn't say white sheep, brown sheep, black sheep, Pentecostal sheep, Charismatic sheep, or Ecumenical sheep. He did not specify old or young, rich or poor. He said, *"My sheep hear My voice, ... and they follow Me."* Period!

Once my wife, Viv, and I were driving through a rural area. There seemed to be cows everywhere, and Viv wanted to see if she could pet one of them. We would slow down and approach them, but about the time she reached out to pet one of the cows, it would bolt and run. We called out to the cows, but they would not come to us.

Then we saw a man parking a pickup truck nearby. He got out and started making some strange noises. I didn't know what he was doing, but suddenly cows were coming from everywhere, running to him. They recognized his voice and knew that in the back of his truck he was carrying food.

Beloved, you were not birthed into the Kingdom of God to be spiritually deaf. In the natural world sometimes children are born deaf. This is not true in the spiritual realm. None was ever born into that realm spiritually deaf. None! You can hear God if you will just be still long enough to listen.

Some of us think we don't have time to hear God. In our instant society, many want answers to their problems today — right now. They want their marriages to be healed and they want their finances to be straightened out, but they don't want to take the time to listen, and they don't want to be disciplined in obeying what God is saying to them. We all want the best life has to offer us, and we want our problems to be solved, and we desire material blessings.

Many are willing enough to come to God for these things, but they don't really want to give God any rights in their lives. They want to be blessed, but they don't want to be saved, born again. They don't want to lay their hearts and lives at the feet of the Savior, Jesus Christ. The only problem with this is that God has no obligation to speak to the unsaved. He often does anyway, out of His love and His grace, but He is not obligated to do so.

When we are saved, we become a son of God, and every son of God has the privilege of hearing His voice. This is not something we must beg Him for. He wants us to hear His voice, and He wants us to follow Him.

NOT BEING FILLED WITH THE HOLY SPIRIT

The second hindrance to knowing God's guidance is that if we are not filled with the Holy Spirit, it is difficult to discern His voice. The lack of the infilling of the Holy Spirit is not a hindrance to going to Heaven, but it is a hindrance to being guided by the Lord properly and correctly. There are many scriptural teachings on this point. For example:

> *However, when He, the Spirit of truth, has come, He will guide you into all truth; for He will not speak on His own authority, but whatever He hears He will speak; and He will tell you things to come.*
>
> John 16:13

No matter who you are, when you were saved, you were indwelt with the Holy Spirit and sealed to redemption. That measure of the Spirit is given to all who come to the Lord. But there is another experience beyond this one, a baptism of power which imparts the spiritual gifts. This experience is received in a onetime experience or baptism, but many infillings follow as we seek to continually stay full of the Spirit. This is a realm of the Holy Spirit that does more than just seal you to the day of redemption.

There are those who teach that when we are saved, we receive all there is for God to give us. Legally, that's true for us, as it was for Israel. As they stood on the banks of the Jordan River, they could see the Promised Land on the other side. God had said to Joshua and, through him, to the people, "I have given you the land. Here's the deed, paid in full." But God didn't want the people to stand where they were and say, "That's ours! That's good land, isn't it." He wanted them to go in and possess that land. Legally, it was theirs. Experientially, however, it did not become theirs until they crossed over the river and went in to possess it.

God doesn't want you to just look into His Word, see what you have been given and then say, "That's mine," without ever having the benefit of the blessing. If the promises of God are truly for us, then we have the right to possess them and to see them operating in our lives.

The baptism of the Holy Spirit is not an award for anything we have done. We cannot earn it. It is a gift of God's grace, an experience which we seek from the Lord and to which we yield. It is a divine enablement, giving us an edge in this life in every area. It brings with it gifts that will empower us to live the Christian life in victory and to more clearly hear the voice of the Lord.

PRIDE

The third hindrance to receiving guidance from the Lord is pride. The Word of God teaches:

> Good and upright is the LORD;
> Therefore He teaches sinners in the way.
> The humble He guides in justice,
> And the humble He teaches His way.   Psalm 25:8-9

Are you one of the humble? If you are, then God will teach you His way.

We often misunderstand humility or meekness. Meekness is not weakness; it is an indication of a teachable spirit. A meek or a humble person, according to the original Greek language used here, is one who has committed his life into the keeping of another. This is not a weak person in any sense of the word.

Jesus said that He was *"meek and lowly of heart"* (Matthew 11:29), yet He was certainly no cowering weakling. The Bible says that Moses was the meekest man in the earth (see Numbers 12:3). Does that mean that he sat around with a pious look on his face all day? I don't think so. That's not meekness. These were men of strength, purpose and vision. They entrusted their lives into the keeping of Another, and they no longer needed to build themselves up in their own estimation.

Pride can cause any person to become what the Word of God refers to as stiff-necked. That means they cannot or you will not bend, change or take responsibility. Peter wrote:

> *Likewise you younger people, submit yourselves to your elders. Yes, all of you be submissive to one another, and be clothed with humility, for "God resists the proud, but gives grace to the humble." Therefore humble yourselves under the mighty hand of God, that He may exalt you in due time.* 1 Peter 5:5-6

"God resists the proud." How can you find God's guidance if He is resisting you?

Pride will keep you from entering into your Promised Land. It will keep you from coming into your inheritance. Jesus said that the meek, or the humble, would *"inherit the earth"* (Matthew 5:5). What will happen to those who are not meek? Obviously, pride will keep them from their inheritance.

SELF-DECEPTION

The fourth hindrance to being guided by God is self-deception. Jesus said:

> *"If anyone wants to do His will, he shall know concerning the doctrine, whether it is from God or whether I speak on My own authority. He who speaks from himself seeks his own glory; but He who seeks the glory of the One who sent Him is true, and no unrighteousness is in Him."*   John 7:17-18

This is the test Christ gave as to whether His doctrine was of God or of Himself. We must not deceive ourselves. It does us no good to look to the Word of God, the Bible, for guidance if we have no intention of obeying it. We are required to obey what we know to be true. Otherwise, we are deceiving ourselves concerning the seriousness of our intent. If we look for guidance in the Word of God and then begin to argue with that guidance, we might as well stop reading the Bible altogether. In this case, it has become nothing more than just another book to us.

If we read the Word of God and look for guidance in its pages, then we must accept that guidance as from the Lord. We cannot say, "I didn't like this passage. I think we'll just cut it out or rewrite it." You cannot approach the Bible looking for agreement with what you have already determined to do. James taught:

But be doers of the word, and not hearers only, deceiving yourselves. For if anyone is a hearer of the word and not a doer, he is like a man observing his natural face in a mirror; for he observes himself, goes away, and immediately forgets what kind of man he was.   James 1:22-24

This passage explains why so many Christians never seem to change. They walk in the mirror of God's Word constantly and see themselves as God sees them, yet they never seem to do anything about it. They walk on unchanged.

People like that may tell their preacher week after week, "Great message, Pastor! That was tremendous, just wonderful!" The preacher may be greatly encouraged by such words of praise, but six weeks later he will see no change in those who expressed them.

We want to be those who hear the Word, look into the mirror of the Word, see where we need to change, and do something about it. Otherwise we are deceiving ourselves. What we are doing with the Word of God and what we are letting the Word of God do in us are equally important.

God wants us to grow up. He wants us to be capable of governing ourselves by allowing the Word we hear to be applied to our lives. If we are to continue to grow and mature, we need the Lord's guidance in many areas. If we think it is not so, we are deceiving ourselves.

It is amazing to me how many people can attend church services week after week and still believe that the messages preached are for everyone there except them. They remind me of the story of the man who came to church faithfully. Every week, he said to the pastor,

Hindrances to Guidance

"Pastor, you sure got 'em today, didn't you?" Sunday after Sunday, he had the same response.

When the area suffered a severe snowstorm, the pastor fought through the snow to get to church, even though the roads were quickly closing. He thought perhaps no one else would come, but suddenly the doors opened and that old fellow came in. They waited a while, but when no one else came, they started the service alone. The preacher was glad, for he was thinking, *This is my opportunity. Now, let's hear him say, 'You got them this morning,'* so he preached like a house on fire. When he got through with the service that morning, the brother came up to him and said, "Well, Preacher, if they'd been here, you would have got 'em this morning!" Too many of us are just like that man. We must take the Word of God to our own hearts and allow it to change us. Self-deception will get us nowhere.

DISHONESTY

The fifth hindrance to hearing God's guidance is dishonesty, a lack of integrity. The book of Proverbs contains a very important verse concerning this sin:

The integrity of the upright will guide them,
But the perversity of the unfaithful will destroy them.
                                              Proverbs 11:3

Beloved, many decisions concerning the will of God are fairly simple. They touch on issues of integrity, of doing what is right, of doing what is honest, of paying your brother what you owe him. If you make a promise or a commitment, then honor what you have said. If you told someone you will be somewhere, be there. If you told someone you would do something, do it. When you make a promise, walk in integrity, walk in honesty, and keep your word. Then you can be guided by God.

There are many other ways in which we, as Christians, fail to walk in integrity, and it presents a very poor testimony to those around us. A Christian man I know once went to a contractor to ask for a job. The contractor's response was, "I'm not hiring any Christians. You can't depend on them." What a commentary on Christian integrity!

When we sin in these ways, through a lack of integrity, it causes people to stumble, for they are watching us. We are called to be *"salt"* (Matthew 5:13) and to be *"light"* (Matthew 5:14) in this world. When we fail in any area of integrity, it robs us of our flavor and of our brightness for our God.

"I've owed my brother for some time now, and I don't know what to do," some say. I know what to do. Pay the man. "But I don't have that much," you might say. Well, then communicate with him and tell him what you will pay each month until the debt is paid. Do the right thing.

God will fight for you, He will defend you, He will uphold you — as long as you are walking in integrity. If you are operating dishonestly, you must fight your battles alone, for God will not be there. If you cannot walk in integrity, you will be forced to walk alone.

REFUSING TO LIVE AN EXAMINED LIFE

The sixth hindrance to guidance is refusing to live an examined life. We must be willing to let others see into our lives and we must have teachable spirits, so that God can correct us. The writer of the Proverbs declared:

> *A man who isolates himself seeks his own desire;*
> *He rages against all wise judgment.* Proverbs 18:1

These are the people who say, "I don't need anyone else." The Word of God is very clear. If we believe that we have no need of others, we are sorely mistaken. We must live open lives among those who can help us to examine ourselves. Those who reject this God-given tool do so to their own peril:

> *... and with all unrighteous deception among those*
> *who perish, because they did not receive the love of*
> *the truth, that they might be saved.*
> 2 Thessalonians 2:10

Are you a lover of the truth? I hope so, for truth must become the measure by which we live. Otherwise, we will be poor guides to those who are watching us to see if what we say lines up with the way we live. Christ said:

> *If the blind leads the blind, both will fall into a ditch.*
> Matthew 15:14

This can happen when we know the truth but do not walk openly in it. Christ prayed to His Father:

> *Sanctify them by Your truth. Your word is truth.*
> John 17:17

If we are too fearful to allow the truth to open our

lives for examination, we cannot receive the guidance of God and know His will. We must be ever-ready to hear and do His Word, because it is truth.

We may not like what we hear sometimes because the truth hurts. I don't like everything God says to me, but it is truth for my life. If we can remain open to obeying the truth, the Holy Spirit will guide us into all truth.

A LACK OF KNOWLEDGE OF THE WORD OF GOD

Another hindrance to walking in God's guidance is a lack of knowledge of His Word. The Bible is the ultimate test of God's guidance, and if we don't know what it says, how are we to discern whether a given course meets with scriptural approval? The Psalmist declared:

Your word is a lamp to my feet
And a light to my path.   Psalm 119:105

God's Word, which guides and directs our steps, is a lamp. It may not show you the entire journey you must travel, and it may not show you long stretches of highway at a time, but it will lead you one step at a time along your journey. It helps you to keep your eyes on God. If it were a searchlight, flooding the entire path with light, you would have no need of walking in faith. It is, rather, a lamp, keeping you close to the Word of God and dependent upon Him always.

Too many Christians today have an opinion about the Bible, but they don't really know the Bible. Knowing the Bible, however, is how we know God, for He is a Spirit. If you want to know His heart, if you want to know His nature, if you want to know His righteousness and His justice, if you want to know how God thinks and feels and what He likes, then you must look into His Word.

A young man in love goes to a friend of his beloved and asks, "What's her favorite kind of flower?" If her favorite is roses, then the young man obviously would never buy her carnations. She might appreciate them as well, but her favorite is roses, so he will buy roses.

The same is true with God. If you want to know about God, read His Word. Then let His Spirit begin to speak to you. If the Spirit says, "He surely likes praise," then you ought to be praising. If the Spirit says, "He sure likes intercession," then begin to intercede. If the Spirit says, "He surely likes to see His people caring for one another," then do it. As we read and study the Bible, we learn to please the One who is most precious and most important to us.

Moses got to know God intimately:

> He made known His ways to Moses,
> His acts to the children of Israel.   Psalm 103:7

All the sons of Israel could see God's acts, but Moses knew God's ways. The others saw the cloud and the pillar; they ate the manna daily; they noticed that their sandals lasted through a forty-year journey; but they never experienced the intimacy Moses enjoyed with God.

It is the same today. If God works a miracle, or if He brings provision, it is not hidden, and all can see it. But not everyone knows God intimately. Not everyone takes time to learn why He does what He does. Knowing God's ways is not just knowing the what; it is also knowing the why. This is a place of intimacy.

God has promised:

I will instruct you and teach you in the way you should go; I will guide you with My eye. Do not be like the horse or like the mule, Which have no understanding, Which must be harnessed with bit and bridle, Else they will not come near you.

Psalm 32:8-9

There are men in my church who are able to read my eyes. They have worked so closely with me through the years that they know what I want at any given time during a service. I can guide them during a service without having to stop and say, "Brother, please go out to the parking lot and see what's going on," or "Brother, please help those people to find seats." Not everyone understands my subtle signals. Some may think I'm just adjusting my glasses or I'm looking strangely at someone, when, in reality, I am guiding with my eyes so that I do not have to disrupt the work of the ministry.

God wants us to be so intimate with Him that we can be guided by His eyes. We are not to be as the stiffnecked, stubborn mule, which must be harnessed and led.

DISOBEDIENCE

Finally, there is no greater hindrance to hearing the voice of God than disobedience. If you have been needing a word from God and you don't seem to be receiving it, consider the possibility that you did not obey Him the last time He spoke to you. If it is true, then this may be the reason He is not speaking to you now. If we have not obeyed the last word God has given us, how can we expect to receive some new word? Obedience is the key to moving on in God.

If any of these hindrances are at work in your life, don't be surprised that you are not hearing God when He speaks to you. Remove the hindrances and you will begin to sense again that God is guiding you daily.

We will now look more closely at each of the seven principles of *God's Guidance System.*

Part II:

The Seven Biblical Principles of Guidance

CHAPTER 3

THE INNER CONVICTION
OF THE SPIRIT

Your ears shall hear a word behind you, saying,
"This is the way, walk in it,"
Whenever you turn to the right hand
Or whenever you turn to the left.   Isaiah 30:21

I know exactly what the prophet was talking about, for it happened to me:

In 1967, when I was traveling and singing with a Gospel quartet, I needed to get to a singing engagement about an hour's drive from where I was preaching that morning. I had a brand new car, a yellow Barracuda. As soon I had finished my service, I jumped in my car, started the engine and was about to pull off when I heard a voice. It said, "Fasten your safety belt." The words were so clearly spoken that I looked over my shoulder to see if someone was there in the back. There was no one. Because the voice had spoken with such authority, I fastened my safety belt before proceeding to the place where our quartet was to sing.

Nothing unusual happened until we had finished singing and I was ready to leave. As I stepped into my vehicle, I again heard that same voice. It had the same authority and spoke with the same clarity: "Fasten your seat belt." I obeyed.

On my way home, I came to a place where I could see the road for a long way. It went straight for a time, then slanted downhill, crossed a bridge and began to go up the other side. There was a large Chrysler in front of me filled with people whom I later learned were returning from a night of drinking and partying. Since the road was so open, I decided to pass them. When I was beside the Chrysler, the driver looked at me and smiled, then swerved suddenly into my lane and crashed into the side of my car. My little Barracuda went spinning round and round, as I went down the hill fighting to get back on the road.

I could see road signs sailing away over the car as I clipped them off, and I could hear metal crunching. It was a while before I was able finally to get the car under control. I later realized that I regained control only because I had my safety belt fastened. If I hadn't fastened my belt when God told me to, I would probably have been killed. Fortunately, I obeyed.

The voice of the Lord, for most of us, is rarely an audible voice. It more often comes in the form of an inner conviction. It is the inward voice of the Holy Spirit.

PAUL WAS GUIDED BY INNER CONVICTION

We see this at work throughout the Word of God. Paul, for instance, was guided by this inner conviction, this inward voice of the Lord:

The Inner Conviction of the Spirit

Now when they had gone through Phrygia and the region of Galatia, they were forbidden by the Holy Spirit to preach the word in Asia. After they had come to Mysia, they tried to go into Bithynia, but the Spirit did not permit them. So passing by Mysia, they came down to Troas. Acts 16:6-8

Paul wanted to take his ministry team to Bithynia, but the Holy Spirit did not permit them to go there. How do you suppose they were prevented from going? I rather imagine that they felt what we call "a check" in their spirits and knew that it was not time yet to go into Asia.

There was nothing wrong with Paul's desire to preach in these places, and that is often our problem. What we want to do is a good thing, but we are not sure if it is God's perfect will for us at that moment. Sometimes God will hold us back, even though what we desire to do is a good thing. The timing is not right.

Paul was moved both by his own inward witness and the inward witness of those with whom he was traveling. God was closing the door, and they all sensed it.

Just as quickly as that door had closed, another one opened. God gave Paul a vision and showed him to go to Troas. For some reason, the trip to Troas was a priority in the heart of God. Paul may not have understood it at the time, but God always knows best.

Some of us fuss and fume whenever it seems God is closing a door to us. We say to God, "I don't understand this. I thought You wanted me to be blessed and to be successful." He does, but He knows better than us how that can be accomplished. He understands what we don't understand. We must never allow ourselves to become so caught up in our own plans — even when they are good plans — that we override the will of God for the moment.

Later, Paul *would* minister in Asia, but he was needed at that particular moment in Troas. God's plan always proves best.

PHILIP WAS GUIDED BY INNER CONVICTION

Another example of guidance by inner conviction is found in the case of Philip:

> *Now an angel of the Lord spoke to Philip, saying, "Arise and go toward the south along the road which goes down from Jerusalem to Gaza." This is desert. So he arose and went.* Acts 8:26-27

Philip was probably looking around him, wondering why God had sent him to this place. Maybe he said, "Here I am, Lord. I'm in the desert, just where You told me to be. Now what am I to do? Why am I here?"

A desert is not usually a place most of us want to visit. Deserts represent barrenness, dryness and thirst. Therefore a desert is a hard place to be, and most of us try to avoid going there. But God knows how to bring life in the desert. If you feel that your life is in a desert place right now, don't be discouraged. God can bring life and purpose into that desert, just as He did for Philip:

> *And behold, a man of Ethiopia, a eunuch of great authority under Candace the queen of the Ethiopians,*

The Inner Conviction of the Spirit

who had charge of all her treasury, and had come to Jerusalem to worship, was returning. And sitting in his chariot, he was reading Isaiah the prophet. Then the Spirit said to Philip, "Go near and overtake this chariot." So Philip ran to him, and heard him reading the prophet Isaiah, and said, "Do you understand what you are reading?" Acts 8:27-30

That scripture reading must have sounded like music to Philip's ears. Here was a foreigner, the Minister of the Treasury to the Ethiopian government, no less, and he was reading the prophet Isaiah. Philip was then able to use that reading to preach Jesus to the man.

Why did Philip accost this official? The Bible says, *"The Spirit said to Philip ..."* The evangelist was bold to approach the Ethiopian official because God told him to do it. And how did the Spirit speak to Philip? Through his inner man, through the inner witness.

There are times when we *do* hear the audible voice of God. Most often, however, when God wants to speak something to us, He begins by speaking Spirit to spirit. Through an inner conviction Philip was guided to preach to this Ethiopian official and was able to lead him to salvation and water baptism.

We see another principle at work here — divine provision. The fact that the Ethiopian was reading the messianic Scriptures found in the writings of Isaiah opened a door for Philip. God had the right man reading the right book at the right time in the right place. He provided Philip with the right opportunity to witness, and Philip took advantage of the opportunity.

God's Guidance System

HOW INNER CONVICTION WORKS

Inner conviction comes to us because the Holy Spirit is in us. He speaks to us, guiding or teaching us. His anointing in us shows us *"all things"*:

> *Little children, it is the last hour; and as you have heard that the Antichrist is coming, even now many antichrists have come, by which we know that it is the last hour. They went out from us, but they were not of us; for if they had been of us, they would have continued with us; but they went out that they might be made manifest, that none of them were of us. But you have an anointing from the Holy One, and you know all things.*
> *And this is the promise that He has promised us eternal life. These things I have written to you concerning those who try to deceive you. But the anointing which you have received from Him abides in you, and you do not need that anyone teach you; but as the same anointing teaches you concerning all things, and is true, and is not a lie, and just as it has taught you, you will abide in Him.*   1 John 2:18-20 and 25-27

The Holy Spirit has sealed us unto the day of redemption (see Ephesians 4:30). I believe this means that we are recreated and the Spirit is instated into our human spirit, writing the Laws of God on the table of our newly softened hearts. God also writes our names in the Lamb's Book of Life, then envelops us with His grace, mercy and eternal love. He puts a sign out for the devil to see. It says, "God's property! No trespassing! Violators will be prosecuted!"

The Inner Conviction of the Spirit

People may not know all this just to look at you. You may look like a normal individual. All of this and more, however, has been accomplished inwardly. You have been anointed inwardly. Through this internal anointing, you have the capacity to know all things that God, through His Holy Spirit, wants you to know — when He wants you to know them.

When you invited Christ into your heart, you gained a capacity for truth, not through any external source, but inwardly, by the Spirit of God. This is for your good. It doesn't make you a know-it-all, but it does assure you that through this anointing you have the potential and the capacity for everything that you need in the realm of knowledge by the Spirit.

How are these things available to you? Through a hearing ear — not your physical ear, but your spiritual ear. Everything you need to know is available to you. So when John said that we have no need for any man to teach us, he was saying, "When I hear truth from God's Word, it will bear witness with the Spirit of truth inside me. What I did not learn in the natural, I now understand by revelation knowledge in my spirit by the Spirit of God."

I can preach Jesus to you, but I cannot reveal Jesus to you. Only the Holy Spirit can do that. No matter what you hear or read or see in the natural, if you truly receive and learn anything, it will be through the work of the Holy Spirit as He confirms what you hear, what you read and what you see. This is how the Spirit teaches us. He quickens, or makes alive to your spirit man, the things which are eternal.

If you learn anything, therefore, it was not from

someone's book or someone's tape or from your pastor. You are taught by God's Spirit, although He uses people to introduce you to each truth.

We must never think, however (as some have to their destruction), that we don't need a pastor or a teacher. This is an unscriptural point of view. If we did not need the ministry gifts, then God would not have placed them into the Body of Christ. Teachers were given to us for the purpose of *"building up of the Body of Christ"* (Ephesians 4:12, NAS), but it is the Spirit of God that is, ultimately, the Teacher. If the Holy Spirit is dwelling within you, then you have the capacity at any moment to know anything that is knowable (if God wants you to know it, and if you are willing to listen).

THE DANGERS OF RELYING SOLELY ON INNER CONVICTION

There is, however, a very real danger in listening only to the voice of the Holy Spirit within and having no other confirmation to that voice. The inner witness of the Holy Spirit is the most mystical and the most subjective of all of the seven principles. Some people begin to think, "Why do I need a map if the One who drew all maps is inside me?" This may sound logical, but it is a totally incorrect position.

Another danger in being moved solely by inner conviction is that we will become proud. Pride has a way of bringing with it deception, until some who think that they are hearing from God are not hearing from God at all.

Some of those who depend only on inner conviction avoid godly counsel. They refuse to sit down with others and hear what they might think. When they do speak with other people they always preface their words with "God told me," thus eliminating any possibility of receiving counsel from others. When we say "God told me," we shut off all further discussion. It's hard to give counsel to someone who already knows everything. None of us is higher than God, and when we begin with the highest authority, saying, "God told me," basically there's nothing left to be said.

God may have told you something, but experience tells me that often either He didn't or else your understanding of what He has said is still limited. By claiming that you know His will already, you cut yourself off from a rich source of wisdom, that which God has invested in His servants.

If you are determined to bypass *God's Guidance System* in order to do something you want to do, you can do it; but don't be surprised when the fruit of your disobedience comes. If you bypass the boundaries God has given to all of us, you cannot then honestly say, "Why did this happen to me? I don't deserve this! I was only looking for truth." If you bypassed *God's Guidance System*, you deserve what you get. God would have protected you if you had only been willing to listen to Him. You weren't looking for truth. If you had been, you would have run through God's checklist before you ever moved forward.

Beloved, we must have ears to hear what the Spirit is saying, but anything that is as subjective as the inner witness of the Holy Spirit must be balanced with other principles of guidance. There is more to guidance, to hearing the word of the Lord, than our feelings, our emotions or our thoughts. Don't believe the lie the enemy wants to pitch your way: "It can't be wrong if it feels so right." Believe me, it can be, and if you are to succeed in the things of God, you will have to grow beyond this limiting mentality.

Just because something feels good doesn't mean it is right. Sin feels good too. Even the Scriptures speak of *"the passing pleasure of sin"* (Hebrews 11:25). We simply cannot afford to be led by our emotions, for, unfortunately, there is still the propensity for sin in each one of us. We are still in fleshly bodies, and we are all recovering from an addiction to sin. This is why God will not lead us by inner conviction alone. We are too apt to go astray.

FALSE GUIDANCE

This is also a very dangerous hour in which we live. John wrote to the churches:

> Little children, it is the last hour; and as you have heard that the Antichrist is coming, even now many antichrists have come, by which we know that it is the last hour.   1 John 2:18

There is another anointing at work in the world, the anointing of antichrist. The term antichrist does not mean "against Christ," as many think, but rather "instead of Christ." The antichrist anointing is a false anointing, a false leading, a false guidance, and if this spirit was at work in John's time, it is even more so today.

The Inner Conviction of the Spirit

How can we identify the antichrist anointing? John wrote:

> *Do not love the world or the things in the world. If anyone loves the world, the love of the Father is not in him. For all that is in the world; the lust of the flesh, the lust of the eyes, and the pride of life; is not of the Father but is of the world.*   1 John 2:15-16

The world is set in opposition to God, and to determine what is of this world, we have a threefold test. If something is of the world, it will be tainted by at least one of these three lusts. *"The lust of the flesh"* speaks of pleasure — physical or emotional. We see this all around us in the endless pursuit of pleasure and excitement that permeates our society. *"The lust of the eyes"* speaks of the desire for possession. This has also permeated our society. We just have to have that new car, that new house, those new clothes, the latest electronic toys. This is a pitfall we, as believers in Christ, must avoid. *"The pride of life"* speaks of a seeking after position, the desire to "make something" of oneself. God made us as it pleased Him, and He continues to desire to form our lives, for He knows what is best for us.

The danger to the Church lies in the fact that these three lusts can counterfeit the true anointing of the Lord. The devil has no new devices, and he doesn't need any. These have been working just fine for him since the very beginning of time. This is why we are warned not to love the things of the world. Each of these temptations can mislead us into feeling that they are from God, because they originate within. They are from an antichrist or an "instead of Christ" leading.

FALSE GUIDANCE IN THE GARDEN

These same temptations were at work in the Garden:

> *Then the serpent said to the woman, "You will not surely die. For God knows that in the day you eat of it your eyes will be opened, and you will be like God, knowing good and evil." So when the woman saw that the tree was good for food, that it was pleasant to the eyes, and a tree desirable to make one wise, she took of its fruit and ate. She also gave to her husband with her, and he ate.* Genesis 3:4-6

Here we see *"the lust of the flesh"* (*"the tree was good for food"*), we see *"the lust of the eyes"* (Eve wanted to possess the fruit of the tree), and we see the boastful *"pride of life,"* the temptation to be *"like God."* What higher position could one ask for?

God is not against pleasure. In fact, *"at [His] right hand are pleasures forevermore"* (Psalm 16:11). He is not against our having possessions. Instead, *"He has pleasure in the prosperity of His servant"* (Psalm 35:27). God is not against position. Why then would the Scriptures declare, *"He who humbles himself will be exalted"* (Matthew 23:12)? No, God is not against any of these things. In fact, through God you can have anything you need to fulfill your destiny.

The problem is that often we want things that are *not* in God's plan for our lives, and if we give place to such desires, we are led right out of the purpose and the destiny of God. Why do we insist on pursuing these things? For our own pleasure, of course, but there is also that niggling feeling, planted in us by the flesh and the devil, that we have no significance without them. We strive to gain these things because we feel as though we're somehow missing something, as though God could not or would not take care of all our needs.

Beloved, if you are one of God's children, then know that your significance, your importance, does not come from anything material or external. It comes from God Himself.

You will not find peace if you look for significance through approval from your pastor, or from any man or woman for that matter. Approval from others is gratifying, but it is no replacement for approval from God. We have been taught to look to man for significance, even within the Church, but this is not what God would have us to do. You are significant in God because you are His, because He made you and because He has a specific destiny for you. You were not an afterthought with God. You are the apple of His eye. How much more significant could you possibly desire to be?

I believe the reason so many Christians are unstable, bouncing from emotion to emotion and from local church to local church, is that they have never learned to get their significance from God.

WRONG MOTIVATIONS

When we are led by the inner conviction, we must constantly examine our motivations. Are we moved by what God is saying to us, or by what we want to hear?

King Saul was not sure that God would bring some-one willing to fight Goliath, so he offered a few incentives of his own:

> *So the men of Israel said, "Have you seen this man who has come up? Surely he has come up to defy Israel; and it shall be that the man who kills him the king will enrich with great riches, will give him his daughter, and give his father's house exemption from taxes in Israel."*   1 Samuel 17:25

Whoever was successful against Goliath was to be given riches and land — possessions which could gratify *"the lust of the eyes."* He would be given the king's daughter, gratifying *"the lust of the flesh."* And he would be exempt from paying the king's tax — a special position, gratifying *"the pride of life."* These were all counterfeit motives set before the warriors to entice them to come forward and fight the giant.

But what was David's motivation when he volunteered to fight Goliath? He said:

> *Who is this uncircumcised Philistine, that he should defy the armies of the living God?*   1 Samuel 17:26

David knew about the rewards Saul was offering, but he was more concerned about the honor of the Name of the Lord, his God.

What are your motives for the things you are doing? Are you driven by pleasure, possession or position? If so, then you are not being led by the Spirit of God, and you are not walking as a child of God in that area of your life.

The Inner Conviction of the Spirit

Are you being motivated by the Holy Spirit? Are you being led by Him? I trust that you can answer yes.

I see this problem of motivation frequently, because of living on Maui. Pastors sometimes call me to say, "I feel led to come to your church to speak for about a week. I will need you to rent a condominium for me and my wife and a car for us to use while we are there." Basically, what they're saying is, "I feel led to have a vacation, and I want your church to pay for it." This is not true of everyone who wants to come out here, but it happens often enough. It's surprising how easily we can sometimes tell what is motivating someone else when they think they are being led by God. Each of us must be sensitive and use discernment to find out what motivates us.

I believe that our motive is more important to God than what we are actually doing. God uses motive, and the devil uses it, too. This can be such a subtle deception, since our motivation flows forth from our inner man. We can so easily deceive ourselves when we want to be deceived.

JESUS WAS ALSO TEMPTED IN THIS REGARD

These three areas of lust can be seen in the temptation of Jesus. He had been baptized by John in the River Jordan and filled with the Holy Spirit by the Father. Then He was driven by the Holy Spirit into the wilderness, and there He fasted for forty days. What stands out to us is that the first voice Jesus heard at the end of His forty-day fast was not God's voice; it was Satan's. Satan was trying to tempt Christ with the same three temptations he has used since he tempted Adam in the Garden.

First, Satan wanted Jesus to turn stones into bread. This was the lure of pleasure or *"the lust of the flesh."*

Next, Satan showed Jesus the kingdoms of the world and offered them to Him if He would only bow down and worship him. This was *"the lust of the eyes,"* the desire for possession. It is not only the desire for possession of something; it is also the glory of having it. Many people desire designer clothing or expensive jewelry because of the glory they obtain through it. I am certainly not against people having nice things, even expensive things. Have all that God will bless you to have, but know the motives of your heart, and do not allow yourself to be entrapped by things which will eventually perish.

Jesus, of course, refused to bow to the devil in this regard, and we must do the same. We must come to the place that we can say, "I will not bow down. I will not violate my purpose. I will not violate my destiny or the will of God for my life just to have some temporary thing of this world." Jesus' basic teaching on life was not what we could acquire, but what we could become.

Finally, Satan took Christ to the pinnacle, the roof of the Temple, and told Him to jump off, since God would protect Him. This was nothing more than *"the pride of life."* "If You will do this, Jesus," Satan was saying, "it will demonstrate Your position. Then everyone will know that You are really the Son of God. All the people will then recognize You and look up to You."

How is it that the young members of the street gangs that thrive in our large cities can be so cold-blooded? It is because they hope to gain the respect of their peers. They want to be somebody.

Jesus didn't have to jump off of the Temple roof because He already knew who He was without having to do anything to prove it or to feel He was accepted by God. You have nothing to prove, either. You are somebody. You have been created in the likeness of God. You have been called *"the righteousness of God in [Christ Jesus]"* (2 Corinthians 5:21). If you feel that you constantly have to prove yourself, then you don't yet know who you are in Christ, and you are in bondage. Search the Scriptures to see who you are in Him ... and who He is in you.

Every fallen believer has had one or more of these three lusts operating in their lives, and every one of them has run through red light after red light before they finally self-destructed for going against God's guidance. There can be no exception to this rule. Those who insist on having their own way in life are on a sure road to loss.

Inner conviction is a good thing. It is a gift from the Lord, but because of who we are and because of the sin that still dwells within us, inner conviction of the spirit cannot stand alone as the only guideline for the decisions of our lives. If you can understand this, then you can avoid the pitfalls that await you.

Thank God for the inner witness of the Holy Spirit. Use it, but use it within the context of the entirety of *God's Guidance System.*

CHAPTER 4

THE SCRIPTURES

The entrance of Your words gives light;
It gives understanding to the simple.

Psalm 119:130

One of the balances we need, when being led by the inner voice, is being led by the Word of God, the Bible. What the Bible says is not based on our emotions, on our mood, or on the stability of our souls. It is unchanging and objective truth. The writer of Proverbs declared:

My son, keep your father's command,
And do not forsake the law of your mother.
Bind them continually upon your heart;
Tie them around your neck.
When you roam, they will lead you;
When you sleep, they will keep you;
And when you awake, they will speak with you.
For the commandment is a lamp,
And the law a light;
Reproofs of instruction are the way of life.

Proverbs 6:20-23

God's Guidance System

The Law of the Lord is a light, a lamp, as we have seen. Why do we need lamps and lights? Because we live in a world of darkness. No matter how brightly the natural sun may be shining, there is much darkness about us in the spiritual realm. We need the light and the lamp of God's Word if we are to see clearly the path we travel. Isaiah foretold:

> *The people who sat in darkness have seen a great light,*
> *And upon those who sat in the region and shadow of*
> *death Light has dawned.* Matthew 4:16

The devil is a liar, and always has been (see John 8:44). He is out to deceive whomever he can. Unfortunately, he is often successful. But that doesn't mean he has to be successful with you. God has given you a lamp and a light to illuminate the darkness, that you may not stumble or lose your way.

Please understand me. I do not seek to nullify the part the Spirit plays in our guidance. We cannot do without Him and His ministry in our lives. But we need to understand that the Spirit will do nothing apart from the Word. The Word does not work without the Spirit, and the Spirit does not work without the Word. You may not always have a clear, specific scripture verse for each situation, but God does give us principles and patterns from the Word of God.

THE SPIRIT AND THE WORD AGREE

There is always agreement between the written Word of God and the Holy Spirit. This never changes. God will never lead you by His Spirit to do anything not in agreement with the Bible. If you are truly being led by the Spirit, somewhere in the Bible you will find an agreement with the way the Spirit of the Lord is leading you. You will never find disagreement. The Spirit and the Word always work in perfect harmony.

Therefore, the most basic test of anything we believe we are hearing from God, would be, Can we find it in the Bible? The Holy Spirit was there even *"in the beginning"*:

> *In the beginning God created the heavens and the earth. The earth was without form, and void; and darkness was on the face of the deep. And the Spirit of God was hovering over the face of the waters.*
> Genesis 1:1-2

The Holy Spirit was *"hovering over the face of the waters."* Another way of translating this is, "brooding over a created world that is without order." The world was there, already created, but there was no order to it yet. The Holy Spirit was there, hovering (or brooding) over the world.

God's desire was to invade this world of chaos and to bring order to it, but how would He do that? The next verse shows us the beginning of a pattern:

> *Then God said, "Let there be light"; and there was light.* Genesis 1:3

The Spirit and the Word were working together from earliest times to impact the natural physical realm. The

Spirit was brooding over the deep waters. Then, through the working together of the Spirit and the Word creation was begun!

When it came time for the creation of man, the record shows:

> *And the LORD God formed man of the dust of the ground, and breathed into his nostrils the breath of life; and man became a living being.*   Genesis 2:7

What was that *"breath of life"* that was breathed into man? It was the very Spirit of God. The Word agreed with the Spirit to create the Earth, and the Spirit agreed with the Word to create man *"a living being."* From the beginning, the Word and the Spirit agreed together. They worked together to accomplish the will of God upon the Earth. It remains so even today.

When you begin to follow God, some people will always say, "Just be led by the Spirit," and there's nothing wrong with that. By the same token, others will always say, "Just follow the Word," and there's nothing wrong with that either. But they are each only part of what we are to do if we are to find our destiny in the Lord. God says, "Follow My Word *and* My Spirit, making sure that the two agree."

You may have heard a saying that begins, "If you're all Word and no Spirit, you dry up." What does this mean? Simply that if you major on the Bible alone, you will become a Pharisee. You may become legalistic and mean-spirited and begin to walk in arrogance because of your knowledge of the Word. When this happens, you begin to wield the Word of God as a weapon — not against the enemy, but against your brothers and sisters. You begin to use it to cut at anyone who dares to cross your path. Why does this happen? Because without the Spirit there is no life.

That saying continues: "If you're all Spirit and no Word, you'll blow up." In other words, you may eventually self-destruct because you acknowledge no parameters within which to bring order. Instead you will face continual confusion. You may be seeing things, hearing things and believing things as truth that God never gave you. You must have the parameters that the written Word contains. Otherwise, you become wise in your own estimation, puffed up with your supposed spirituality.

The conclusion to this saying is, "But with Spirit and Word you'll grow up." This is so true! We do not have to choose one or the other. We need both, in the proper balance and in harmony, if we want to grow into mature Christians who not only have life in us, but who have order in that life as well.

God gave a warning to those who looked only to the Spirit, without being knowledgeable concerning the Scriptures:

> *And the word of the LORD came to me, saying, "Son of man, prophesy against the prophets of Israel who prophesy, and say to those who prophesy out of their own heart, 'Hear the word of the LORD!' " Thus says the Lord GOD: "Woe to the foolish prophets, who follow their own spirit and have seen nothing!"*
> Ezekiel 13:1-3

God's Guidance System

Each of us must be solidly grounded in the Scriptures, and each of us must learn discernment in the spiritual realm. We cannot accept guidance that comes totally apart from the Bible, for this Book has been given to us by God for our benefit.

We cannot benefit, however, from God's Word, if we fail to take the time and make the effort to read and study it. I am always concerned about immature Christians who are susceptible to the spiritual realm, but who do not yet know the Word well enough to guide them, to keep them and to give them boundaries. What is frightening is that even those who have been saved for a while are often lacking in this area. When this is the case, anyone might come along, showing off a supernatural gift, even using a familiar spirit which is not of God, and lead such people into deception.

We need to know the Word of God. God expects us to get into the Spirit, and He expects us to get into the Word. He expects us to make these two our principle guidance system.

Never will God stray outside the boundaries of His Word. Never will He do anything contrary to His Spirit. Together, these are two of your most dependable witnesses or principles, and the two of them underlie each of the others.

THE BALANCE OF SPIRIT AND WORD

Jesus spoke of the Word and the Spirit, and of how both are needed:

And no one puts new wine into old wineskins; or else

The Scriptures

the new wine bursts the wineskins, the wine is spilled,
and the wineskins are ruined. But new wine must be
put into new wineskins. Mark 2:22

In this illustration, the Word corresponds to the wineskin. A wineskin holds the wine; it doesn't produce it. The new wine that Jesus spoke of here corresponds to the Holy Spirit. What is it about the Holy Spirit that is different than the wineskin? The wine is alive. It's bubbly, effervescent, free. It's flowing, moving.

If the wine has nothing to contain it, however, it will quickly be dispersed and be wasted. It must be put into a wineskin. This is a powerful teaching.

If the wineskins of the New Testament time were not kept flexible, by regular oiling, they would eventually burst. It was good for us to learn foundational things. We need them. But we cannot stop with what we learned years ago, what we saw months ago, what was taught to us last week. We need to keep our wineskins well oiled. We need to maintain them. We need to get into the Word and get the Word into us. If we do that, our wineskin will remain strong and full of life.

Although there is only one baptism of the Holy Spirit, there are many fillings. Each one of these fillings needs to be more intense, more alive, greater, deeper and higher than the previous experience. If the wineskin is allowed to remain in the same condition, without changing, it will burst, and you will lose everything.

We have quite a few broken wineskins in the Church. They no longer hold any life. They merely parrot what they have learned in the Bible through the years. They are merely an echo and not a voice. Even the Word of

God has no life for them, because their wine is gone. Their life has been spilled out and wasted. Nothing of significance will be produced by such people as long as they exist in that state.

Beloved, if the wine is to find its true expression, it cannot be left to itself. It must come inside some structure where it can be maintained. The wine will not lose its life simply because we put it into a structure.

Some people seem to be fearful of having any guidelines within a meeting, or of having any parameters for sharing a word from the Lord. But God's life is stronger than that! It will not die simply because we place guidelines upon its use. God wants things to be done in order, not in chaos. Paul wrote:

> *Therefore, brethren, desire earnestly to prophesy, and do not forbid to speak with tongues. Let all things be done decently and in order.*
>
> 1 Corinthians 14:39-40

Because a word is not acted upon immediately does not mean that it is being disregarded. It may be set aside as we seek the Lord's leading concerning the proper timing of it. This is not quenching the Spirit, but rather using wisdom in the application of what God is saying to His people.

There are parameters in which the Spirit can operate without bringing confusion into the Body of Christ. It does no harm to the Spirit to put Him into the confines of the Word. What that does is to give life to the Word.

It is true that we are instructed not to *"quench the Spirit"*:

The Scriptures

Do not quench the Spirit.   1 Thessalonians 5:19

When we think of quenching something, we usually think of putting it out, the way we would blow out the flame of a candle. That, however, is not what is meant here by quenching. What it actually means is "to subdue or suppress." Unfortunately, many believers subdue or suppress the work of the Holy Spirit in their lives. They may be ready to move forward when the enemy slithers in and says, "You may be out of order, you know." If we know the Word of God and allow it to have its way in our lives, then we will be able to discern whether or not we are out of order, and we will be able to move on in God — regardless of what the enemy has to say about it.

EARTHEN VESSELS

The Word of God declares:

We have this treasure in earthen vessels.
                                    2 Corinthians 4:7

Because we have the treasure of God *"in earthen vessels,"* you may very well be out of order sometimes. You may move into the flesh sometimes. We judge a message, however, by its content, not by the humanness of the messenger.

Suppose you go outside on a hot summer day, and you water your lawn with a hose. It's hot and the sun is beating down on your head, and you decide you want a drink of that cold water. You take a drink from the hose, and what does that water taste like? It tastes like the hose, doesn't it? It's still water. It's still life. It's still able to cause the grass to grow. It's still able to sustain and keep you. Yet it tastes like the hose. Why? Because it's coming out of that hose.

It's the same way with the Holy Spirit flowing from us. Not every "Thus saith the Lord" will sound like it's coming directly from the throne room of God. Some of what we say will have our personality in it. We are still earthen vessels, even though we are in the process of being changed, as we behold His face. Therefore, please do not judge yourself or your brother or your sister; judge the content of the message. Does it match up with what the Spirit is saying through others? Does it match up with the Bible? If so, then receive it, and just rinse the taste of the hose from your mouth.

Just because we carry this treasure in earthen vessels, God doesn't want us to quench or to suppress the Holy Spirit. He doesn't want us to subdue Him. He simply wants us to keep the Spirit of the Lord in conjunction with the Word and the Word in conjunction with the Spirit.

A RELEASE OF DIRECTION

There are three things that are released when the Holy Spirit operates within the structure of the Word. The first is a release of direction. Don't you hate being lost? It can be confusing; it can be scary; it can be dangerous (if you end up in the wrong place); and it can be costly before you get back on the right road. God wants to spare us of all that by giving us direction.

The Scriptures

It's good to know where you're going, and many Christians *seem* to know. They say, "I'm being led by the Spirit," but if we ask them where they are going, they have no idea. They have no idea of their destiny or purpose, despite the fact that God wants us to know these things! How can we do or be what He created us to do and to be if we don't have any idea of what that is?

What is your purpose? What is your destiny? What has God called you to do? What is God saying to you? Those who have no direction in God will respond, "I don't really know. I'm just waiting on God." Beloved, we waste a lot of time "waiting on God" simply because we don't know how God guides. Waiting on God is good and necessary ... in its place, but too often we are content to sit and wait long after God wants us to get on the road. Allow God to give you a release of direction for your life.

A Sense of Focus

The second thing you will receive when you allow the Holy Spirit to operate within the structure of the Word is a sense of focus. Just as a camera needs to be properly focused in order to take a sharp, clear picture, so we need a focus, a clarity of vision, if we are to see what God has for us to do. Most of us, when we begin to see a vague outline — men walking about like trees — think we already have the full picture. We have a general idea, but we really do not see the vision God has for us clearly enough to be totally effective.

We try to move forward in the purposes of God before they are even fully formed in our own minds.

Despite the fact that we don't yet understand, we are eager to push ahead.

God wants us to be able to see clearly, to have a clear focus, and when the Word and the Spirit work together, we can have that clear focus on life. The shady areas will melt away, and we will know exactly where we are going.

AN IMPACT OR IMPARTATION

The third thing that happens when we allow the Word and Spirit to work together is an impact or impartation. We suddenly find that we are having an impact on whatever it is that we are involved with. Why? Because of the impartation we have received through the Word and through the Spirit.

Thus, we will know where we are going, we will know what to do when we get there, and the result will be that in that particular area we will see God's will being done *"on Earth as it is in Heaven."* What more could we ask for? This is the measure of success God wants to see visited upon our lives and our ministries.

JESUS IS THE WORD!

Jesus is the Word:

In the beginning was the Word, and the Word was with God, and the Word was God.
And the Word became flesh and dwelt among us, and we beheld His glory, the glory as of the only begotten of the Father, full of grace and truth.

John 1:1 and 14

The Scriptures

The Word was made alive and was walking the Earth in the form of Jesus Christ. For the first thirty years of His life here on Earth, however, Jesus did no miracles. He was a good Carpenter; He was a good Son; He was a good Jewish citizen; He did everything that was expected of Him; but He did no miracles. That, however, did not nullify the fact that He was the Word. Nothing could change that fact.

Jesus did not minister at all before He was baptized with the Spirit. There is no record of His ministry until after He was baptized in water by John the Baptist, and the Holy Spirit came upon Him. The Word did not work any miracles without the Spirit.

The fact that you have heard something in the Spirit — an inner conviction — or that you have received a prophetic word does not cause anything to happen in your life. People often say, "Oh, I went to that meeting and I got a word." Sometimes we hold onto those words for years before anything happens.

I know. I've gotten words, and I've given words to others, but getting a word does not make something happen. It takes the word and the Spirit working together to bring to pass whatever is on God's heart to do. The two do not work separately from one another. If you have the Word in you and you have the Spirit in you, then you have the potential to walk just like Jesus walked:

How God anointed Jesus of Nazareth with the Holy Spirit and with power, who went about doing good and healing all who were oppressed by the devil, for God was with Him. Acts 10:38

How was Christ able to do all that He did while He walked the Earth? He said:

> *"When you lift up the Son of Man, then you will know that I am He, and that I do nothing of Myself; but as My Father taught Me, I speak these things. And He who sent Me is with Me. The Father has not left Me alone, for I always do those things that please Him."*
>
> John 8:28-29

Jesus was saying, "I'm not free-lancing!" He did the things that pleased His Father. He worked within the parameters of the Word and the Spirit, at the direction of the Father. When the Father directed Jesus, the Word (that which He is) and the Spirit (that which is within Him) came together in agreement to accomplish whatever the Father desired. So the guidance of the Spirit in Jesus was limited to the Father's will, nature, character and personality.

Jesus never violated the Word. He tore tradition asunder, but He never violated the Word. That is why the Pharisees were so infuriated with Him. They could never find Him guilty of any violation of the Word, while, at the same time, He trampled on their most endearing traditions.

Now, in the dawning days of a new century, the Holy Spirit is still in perfect agreement with the Word. The Spirit still hovers, brooding, confirming and bringing to pass the things written in the Word and spoken by the Word.

When the Word and the Spirit come into agreement and stay in agreement, something is created. There is a miracle. There is an incredible expression of life. We cannot, however, try to force the hand of the Lord or try to move ahead of Him on the basis of a single witness. We cannot move into some new area saying, "I felt led." We must examine what the Word of God has to say about the matter. If the Word is in agreement with what we are feeling, we may be on the right track. If the Word and what we feel agree, then we have two witnesses.

The more we read the Word of God, the more we see how the Father does what He does. The Word reveals Him; it reveals His nature and His character. If we are spending time in the Bible, we will not have to wonder who God is, how He acts, what He wants. It's all there. Our part is to be faithful to read, to study, to memorize, to discover the treasures within the Word.

We do not read the Bible to validate what we want to do. We read the Bible to find out who God is, what He wants to do and how we fit into that picture. The Scriptures thus become our wineskin, giving definition to the expression of the Holy Spirit in our lives.

When we are solid in the Bible, when it is time to move, we will move, and when it's time to act, we will act, but we will act within the guidelines of the Word. There will be no confusion or destruction or violence. Life will flow forth from our actions.

THE FRUIT OF REBELLION

Some people say, "I know that God wants me to do something. I just don't know what it is. I'm just so confused." What does this mean, and how can we help? Either this person does not know a scripture, a principle or a moral pattern, which they can learn through godly help and counsel, or he does not want to make the hard choice to act on what the Word has already clearly defined for him.

Some people go through life moving from local church to local church, looking for a second opinion, then a third, then a fourth. They look for someone who will refute what God is saying to them, rather than simply being obedient to walk in what God has shown them. Why do people do this? Because of fear. They are afraid to change. But making that simple change would allow the Spirit of God to work in that person's life to bring him into the purposes of God.

The Word must be working mightily within each one of us. How successful we are in obtaining God's guidance in our lives will be in direct relation to our knowledge of the Word. People who know the Word make fewer mistakes in knowing God's will, for the Word *"gives light."*

When we need understanding, we know where to go to get that understanding. We get it from the Word of God in conjunction with the Spirit:

> *How can a young man cleanse his way?*
> *By taking heed according to Your word.*
> *With my whole heart I have sought You;*
> *Oh, let me not wander from Your commandments!*
> *Your word I have hidden in my heart,*
> *That I might not sin against You.*
>
> Psalm 119:9-11

If we choose to follow it, the Word of God will lead

us into paths of righteousness. Knowledge of the Scriptures will produce in us a pure life, pleasing to God. Through His Word, God can lead us gently, guiding us so that we do not *wander from [His] commandments.* If, however, we have neglected to hide the Word in our hearts, there is no way we can be successfully led by the Spirit. Instead, we will follow emotions, feelings, the advice of friends, human logic or knowledge.

Every time we sense the inner leading of the Lord, the first thing we should look for is scriptural confirmation. You might pray, "Lord, show it to me in Your Word" or "God, prove it to me from the Bible." The Lord may give you a specific verse, or He may show you a recurring principle in the Bible that applies to your situation.

Even when using the Bible, pray for wisdom. Ideally, you should find a balance of truth running through several scriptural texts, not just a single verse. Decisions should not be based on a single "proof text."

Beloved, get into the Word, and get the Word into you. Pick that Bible up from the shelf and get it into your heart. That is the key to success in this life, and in the world to come. Letting the Word be your guide is an important principle of *God's Guidance System.*

CHAPTER 5

PROPHECY

Do not despise prophecies. Test all things; hold fast what is good.   1 Thessalonians 5:20-21

The third witness of *God's Guidance System* is prophetic utterance, one of the ways God has chosen to speak to His people in this New Testament era, and we are not to despise it. It is one of the gifts of the Spirit God has placed in the Body of Christ for our edification:

But the manifestation of the Spirit is given to each one for the profit of all ... to another prophecy.
1 Corinthians 12:7 and 10

Prophecy is a word from God given to a believer or a group of believers through a fellow believer. There may be times, and there often are, when the gift of prophecy is used along with another spiritual gift. For example, a word of wisdom or a word of knowledge may be used prophetically to bring the word of the Lord to an individual.

It is important to note that according to the Scriptures, prophecy is given *"for the profit of all."* It is for the benefit and guidance of each individual, so that the Body of Christ as a whole may prosper.

God's Guidance System

PAUL RECEIVED PROPHECY

The following example of prophetic guidance is found in the life of St. Paul:

> *From Miletus he [Paul] sent to Ephesus and called for the elders of the church. And when they had come to him, he said to them: "You know, from the first day that I came to Asia, in what manner I always lived among you, serving the Lord with all humility, with many tears and trials ... .*
> *And see, now I go bound in the spirit to Jerusalem, not knowing the things that will happen to me there, except that the Holy Spirit testifies in every city, saying that chains and tribulations await me. But none of these things move me; nor do I count my life dear to myself, so that I may finish my race with joy, and the ministry which I received from the Lord Jesus, to testify to the gospel of the grace of God."*
> Acts 20:17-19 and 22-24

Paul had set his face toward Jerusalem, and he was receiving prophetic confirmations of God's will for his life all along the way. He knew that these words were from God, and they were to help prepare him for what he would have to face in the Holy City.

The prophetic word was the same wherever Paul went: *"Chains and tribulations await [you]."* He knew that he had been led by the Spirit to go to Jerusalem, but he had not known exactly what he would face there. Along the way, God was revealing it to him through individual prophecies given by various believers. What an exciting journey that must have been!

Prophecy

I wonder how many of us would have continued the journey if we had been receiving warnings like these. It is always difficult to face hardships, but when we are forewarned by the Holy Spirit, we are able to prepare ourselves for any eventuality. If God knows exactly what we are about to face, then we can be sure that He will be with us through the trial.

One of the best parts of facing any trial is to know that it will pass, as others have. Trials are not permanent in our lives, but the presence of God is. With His presence in our lives, we can pass through every trial and we do it in His strength. This is part of how we grow and mature, so that we can become more effective for the Kingdom of God.

As Paul continued his journey, the message of the Spirit to him continued to be confirmed. Because of this, some even tried to persuade him not to go to Jerusalem. Paul, however, could not be persuaded. He must reach Jerusalem. Some have suggested that Paul was being disobedient to God by insisting on continuing his journey, but that can't be true. The message of the Spirit to him was clear. Those who tried to dissuade him from going were doing so out of their great love for him as a person. He was their spiritual father, and in their hearts they were afraid of what would happen to him if he went to Jerusalem.

When Paul reached Caesarea, the prophetic warnings continued, this time in a new way:

And as we stayed many days, a certain prophet named Agabus came down from Judea. When he had come to us, he took Paul's belt, bound his own hands and feet, and said, "Thus says the Holy Spirit, 'So shall the Jews at Jerusalem bind the man who owns this belt, and deliver him into the hands of the Gentiles.' " Now when we heard these things, both we and those from that place pleaded with him not to go up to Jerusalem. Then Paul answered, "What do you mean by weeping and breaking my heart? For I am ready not only to be bound, but also to die at Jerusalem for the name of the Lord Jesus." Acts 21:10-13

Often those who love us the most can unwittingly and unknowingly hinder us. They can't always understand where God is leading us and why. It is natural for us to want to spare our loved ones any pain or heartache, and it is natural for them to suggest that we spare ourselves. Sometimes, however, we must pass through difficulties if we are to truly follow the Lord; sometimes we must pay the price to be a true disciple; and sometimes what seems to promise us the most pain is, in actuality, the place where we will meet with the Lord and see His great power at work. Don't fear the place of battle, for it is often the place of greatest victory.

No doubt the things these people were saying and doing were tugging at Paul's heart. They loved him, and he loved them. But he said to them, "What do you mean by weeping and breaking my heart?" He was saying, "Listen, I have received a word from the Lord. I know what my destiny is. I know what God is calling me to and what awaits me in that call, and I am ready for that. I have prepared myself to be obedient. Don't keep crying and breaking my heart. I know you love me. I know you don't want to see me suffer. But, please, beloved, come into agreement with me. Your strength of faith and agreement will do more for me than all of your sympathy."

Paul received and accepted the prophetic words that came forth in city after city. He understood that God was trying to prepare him for what was ahead, so that he would not be surprised by the hardships that awaited him. These prophecies were for his benefit. They were not to frighten him or to hinder him, but to help him.

The prophecies also helped the people along the way, by showing them what Paul was to go through for the sake of the Gospel. How much more fervent their prayers would be for Paul once they understood what awaited him in Jerusalem! How much more they must have planned for his support in every way! These particular prophetic words brought a measure of sorrow for what Paul would suffer, but how much better it is to be ready when sorrow is to be our lot! Prophecy is a valid part of *God's Guidance System.*

THE WORK OF PROPHECY

Most of the work of prophecy can be described in three words: *"edification and exhortation and comfort"*:

> But he who prophesies speaks edification and exhortation and comfort to men.   1 Corinthians 14:3

The New International Version of the Bible calls these three: *"strengthening, encouragement and comfort."* The Holy Spirit is the Comforter. God never destroys. He never divides. He never tears His people down. He always wants to strengthen His Body, and this is the purpose of the gifts He has placed in the Church.

Everything that comes forth from God is redemptive. Even when He must use the rod of discipline on us, it is to redeem His purposes in us. He never corrects us to hurt us or to drive us away from Him. His desire is to enable us to fulfill the destiny and the good purpose that He has for us as individual members and as a corporate Body. Therefore, prophecy is a love-gift from God to the Church, and any gift of God is good.

The Holy Spirit will always bring comfort. He will always edify and encourage and exhort. The end result of all New Testament prophecy is comfort. After all, prophecy is the gift of the One who is the Comforter. Even if there must be scathing rebuke through the prophetic word (which should happen very rarely), the Lord will always point us to repentance and a promise. Why? Because everything in God is redemptive.

That does not mean that God will never bring you to a place of chastisement. He has already told us that He chastens everyone He loves:

> *For whom the LORD loves He chastens, And scourges every son whom He receives. If you endure chastening, God deals with you as with sons; for what son is there whom a father does not chasten? But if you are without chastening, of which all have become partakers, then you are illegitimate and not sons.*
>
> Hebrews 12:6-8

God's chastening is never for destruction. It always leads us to redemption.

Prophecy

THE POTENTIAL FOR ABUSE

Unfortunately, even God's gifts can be misused or abused when they are placed in human hands. Prophecy, because of its nature, seems to be misused more frequently than some of the other gifts of the Spirit. If there is anything in the church that is tearing people down, anything that is manipulating or controlling them, anything that is hurting them, we can know that it has not been energized by the Holy Spirit. This is simply not God's way.

Prophecy is a wonderful gift, and great things have and will come of it. We can gain needed insight through this gift. But, although this is a spectacular and good gift, it can also be the most dangerous of the gifts. When it's right, it's powerful; but when it's wrong, it can be devastating and can leave people shattered. We must be very careful and very serious when we approach this method of guidance.

Because of the opportunity for abuse and misuse, there are some scriptural guidelines given to us by Saint Paul regarding prophecy. Paul was writing to the Church at Corinth to correct some abuses there. The church was misusing their spiritual gifts, and that had opened the door to confusion. They had power and anointing, and the gifts of the Spirit were all in operation in their midst, but they were in some confusion, and there were some who were out of control.

Paul was not writing to the Corinthian church to abolish these gifts. What he was seeking to do was to correct the abuse and misuse.

Again, we see that a wineskin is needed. There is freedom in the use of the gifts, but there must also be structure to contain that freedom and that life. Paul wrote:

> *Pursue love, and desire spiritual gifts, but especially that you may prophesy. For he who speaks in a tongue does not speak to men but to God, for no one understands him; however, in the spirit he speaks mysteries. But he who prophesies speaks edification and exhortation and comfort to men. He who speaks in a tongue edifies himself, but he who prophesies edifies the church. I wish you all spoke with tongues, but even more that you prophesied; for he who prophesies is greater than he who speaks with tongues, unless indeed he interprets, that the church may receive edification.*   1 Corinthians 14:1-5

Paul was contrasting the gifts of speaking in tongues and prophesying. The Church at Corinth apparently had elevated the gift of speaking in tongues beyond its place, so the Apostle was clarifying the purposes and uses of the two gifts. It was then that Paul wrote that prophecy is to edify, exhort and comfort, that words of prophecy are to encourage us, to stir us to do the will of God. He said further:

> *How is it then, brethren? Whenever you come together, each of you has a psalm, has a teaching, has a tongue, has a revelation, has an interpretation. Let all things be done for edification.*
> *Let two or three prophets speak, and let the others judge. But if anything is revealed to another who sits by, let the first keep silent. For you can all prophesy*

Prophecy

one by one, that all may learn and all may be encouraged. And the spirits of the prophets are subject to the prophets. For God is not the author of confusion but of peace, as in all the churches of the saints.

1 Corinthians 14:26 and 29-33

Prophecy must have guidelines, just like other spiritual gifts. One of the first of these guidelines is: *"let two or three prophets speak, and let the others judge."* What does this mean? We are to evaluate the message by the Spirit, having the proper attitude and spirit within ourselves. This is liberty within structure.

The passage does not define which prophecy is to be judged, therefore, all prophecy is to be judged. It does not matter how noted a person may be speaking as a prophet. His or her words are still to be evaluated. A given word, for example, may not be valid for a particular time. It might be something to hold onto for later use. For instance, just because someone gets up and says, "Yea, I say unto you that God is calling you to go to Africa," that doesn't mean you should go home and start packing that very moment. It doesn't mean you are to go to Africa that week, that month or even that year. It simply means that you should begin to examine your heart and your call. And, as always, you should measure this word against other witnesses God has given you.

In the Old Testament there were also specific guidelines in place concerning prophets and their prophecies. If a prophet prophesied, and what he said did not come to pass, he was taken outside the city and stoned. Our guidelines are not quite so harsh! But we do need to evaluate prophecy, since there is always the possibility of error, most notably in timing and interpretation. If God has said something, He will validate it.

Don't misunderstand me. This is not a time to be judging our brothers. As we have seen already, God puts His treasures in earthen vessels and as He said, *"the excellence of the power [is] ... not of us"* (2 Corinthians 4:7). Just disregard the vessel and scoop out the treasures. We are far too consumed with personalities and we dwell far too much on the *"us,"* but, Paul said, *"the power [is] ... not of us."* As a Church we tend to become totally enamored of the latest teaching, the latest prophetic word, the latest popular preacher. But we must learn to look past all of these things to what God is truly trying to speak to each of us.

VALIDATION

In the biblical account of the ten lepers, ten men were crying out to Christ for mercy. He told them to *"go show [them]selves to the priests"*:

> *So when He saw them, He said to them, "Go, show yourselves to the priests." And so it was that as they went, they were cleansed.* Luke 17:14

Why did the lepers need to go and present themselves to the priests? Because the priests functioned as the physicians in cases of leprosy. They diagnosed this disease, they gave the prescription (quarantine) and they were the only ones who could legally declare anyone healed and lift that quarantine. It was the priests who validated the miracle that Christ had done for the ten lepers.

Every healing that Jesus does can be validated. Every miracle that He does can be put to the test. Each one can be substantiated, whether by a medical X ray or by an expert opinion or by whatever other means. God is not afraid of examination. We can evaluate what HE has done, for if God Himself has done a thing, we can rest assured that the saying "He does all things well" is true.

This doesn't bother God. He is not afraid for us to examine a work to see if it is His workmanship. In fact, He expects us to do so, otherwise we might be deceived into accepting things that are not of God as being His works. God gives us wisdom and discernment because He *desires all men ... to come to the knowledge of the truth* (1 Timothy 2:4).

This is an important concept to understand. It does not devalue God's work when we examine it to make sure it is of Him. We are expected to evaluate and validate things in His Kingdom.

No one is infallible, and no one is infallible when it comes to prophecy. No one!

THE OFFICE OF THE PROPHET

It is also important to notice that not everyone who prophesies is a prophet. There is a difference between the gift of prophesying and the office of the prophet. The fact that you may speak forth a prophetic utterance from time to time does not make you a prophet. The spirit of prophecy can come upon anybody at any time as long as spiritual life is allowed to flow through a person unhindered. God can move in this way through any believer who is willing to be a vessel for His use.

God's Guidance System

But there are people who are separated as prophets. They have a special ministry given by God to the Church. Paul wrote:

> *And He Himself gave some to be apostles, some prophets, some evangelists, and some pastors and teachers, for the equipping of the saints for the work of ministry, for the edifying of the body of Christ, till we all come to the unity of the faith and of the knowledge of the Son of God, to a perfect man, to the measure of the stature of the fullness of Christ.* Ephesians 4:11-13

There were prophets in the early days of the New Testament, and there are also prophets today. They are people who have a resident gift of prophecy. They can use this gift at any time, while others can prophesy only when the spirit of prophecy comes upon them.

Concerning the proper use of prophecy in the context of the public meeting of the local church, Paul wrote that there was to be order within the meeting as those who prophesied gave way to one another, for, he said, *"the spirits of the prophets are subject to the prophets. "* He drove that point home by further stating: *"For God is not the author of confusion but of peace, as in all the churches of the saints."*

This is a crucial point. If there is confusion in our midst, there can be no peace. The Word of God also states:

> *And let the peace of God rule in your hearts, to which also you were called in one body; and be thankful.*
> Colossians 3:15

Prophecy

This is the subject of another chapter, so we will not dwell on it here, but suffice it to say that God's desire is that we have peace, and if there is confusion, the Holy Ghost is not responsible for it.

CAN WOMEN PROPHESY?

It is obvious that a prophetic word must come through a believer, that it is better if it comes through a prophet, but that it may come through any Spirit-filled believer. But may a prophetic word come through a woman? Surprisingly, in this enlightened age, this question is often asked. It is because of what Paul taught the Corinthians in that same fourteenth chapter of his first letter:

> *Let your women keep silent in the churches, for they are not permitted to speak; but they are to be submissive, as the law also says. And if they want to learn something, let them ask their own husbands at home; for it is shameful for women to speak in church.*
>
> 1 Corinthians 14:34-35

Some churches use these two verses to prevent women from preaching or teaching and even from prophesying in the church. This is a tragic misinterpretation of scripture. These verses must not be lifted out of context. The basic tenets of the Scriptures can be found in many places, usually not just one. I am afraid that it has been the delight of machistic, egotistic and legalistic men to use these verses to prevent spiritually strong women from finding their rightful place in the Church.

If women could not prophesy, then why would Paul write that a woman could prophesy as long as she was covered?

> *But every woman who prays or prophesies with her head uncovered dishonors her head, for that is one and the same as if her head were shaved.*
>
> 1 Corinthians 11:5

And what of the daughters of Philip the Evangelist who prophesied?

> *On the next day we who were Paul's companions departed and came to Caesarea, and entered the house of Philip the evangelist, who was one of the seven, and stayed with him. Now this man had four virgin daughters who prophesied.* Acts 21:8-9

And what of Elizabeth's prophetic greeting of Mary or of the prophetess Anna who spent so much time in the Temple and helped to introduce the Savior to the nation of Israel? Obviously, there is something wrong with a teaching that prohibits women from prophesying.

We can begin to understand what Paul was saying to the Corinthian church in these verses if we recognize that Jewish tradition put severe restrictions on women. Until New Testament times, Hebrew women had few rights. Paul, therefore, was saying, "Your tradition says, 'let your women keep silent in the church.' " He then continued:

Or did the word of God come originally from you?
Or was it you only that it reached?

1 Corinthians 14:36

In other words, Paul was asking, "Did you write the Book? Are your traditions to be considered coequal with the Holy Scriptures?" They had tried to keep women in the limited sphere of being wives and mothers and workers, but suddenly, by the blood of Jesus Christ and the coming of the Holy Spirit, women had been released into a beautiful and dignified liberty. Paul was attempting to correct the confusion that had arisen from ancient traditions. He was certainly not teaching the church leaders to silence their women.

The only exception to this teaching is found in Paul's letter to Timothy:

And I do not permit a woman to teach or to have authority over a man, but to be in silence.

1 Timothy 2:12

Women are not *"to have authority over a man."* There is no biblical pattern to support a woman governing men. Women may, however, occupy positions of leadership within the church, and they may operate in the spiritual gifts. So women may prophesy, just as men can. Gender has nothing to do with it. The message is the important thing.

DIRECTIONAL PROPHECY

There are several different types of prophecy, and any one of them may be used in the area of guidance. The first type of prophecy is directional prophecy. This type of prophecy, more frequently seen in Old Testament times, is rare in our time, although it does occur.

Just after the prophet Samuel had anointed Saul to be king, he gave him a very detailed directional prophecy:

> *"When you have departed from me today, you will find two men by Rachel's tomb in the territory of Benjamin at Zelzah; and they will [speak] to you ... .*
>
> *"Then you shall go on forward from there and come to the terebinth tree of Tabor. There three men going up to God at Bethel will meet you, one carrying three young goats, another carrying three loaves of bread, and another carrying a skin of wine. And they will greet you and give you two loaves of bread, which you shall receive from their hands.*
>
> *"After that you shall come to the hill of God where the Philistine garrison is. And it will happen, when you have come there to the city, that you will meet a group of prophets coming down from the high place with a stringed instrument, a tambourine, a flute, and a harp before them; and they will be prophesying. Then the Spirit of the LORD will come upon you, and you will prophesy with them and be turned into another man. And let it be, when these signs come to you, that you do as the occasion demands; for God is with you.*
>
> *"You shall go down before me to Gilgal; and surely I will come down to you to offer burnt offerings and make sacrifices of peace offerings. Seven days you shall wait, till I come to you and show you what you should do."*

Prophecy

So it was, when he had turned his back to go from Samuel, that God gave him another heart; and all those signs came to pass that day.   1 Samuel 10:2-9

It was as though Samuel had drawn a map for Saul. The directions were just that clear, just that detailed. Why is this type of prophecy a rarity in New Testament times? Because God no longer lives in a Tabernacle or Temple; He dwells in our hearts. He expects us to be guided and led by His Spirit in us, not through an external such as a directional prophecy. This type of prophecy does occur today, but when it does, we must be cautious and look for other witnesses to confirm it.

CONFERRAL PROPHECY

The second type of prophecy is conferral prophecy. This is prophecy that confers something to the one receiving the word. It gives, grants, bestows or imparts:

Do not neglect the gift that is in you, which was given to you by prophecy with the laying on of the hands of the eldership [presbytery].   1 Timothy 4:14

This conferral type of prophecy is often a prophetic ministry, and is most often used as it was for Timothy. In these cases, a gifting is imparted through the laying on of hands by the presbytery, eldership or other church governmental leadership, with prophecy spoken forth. The gifting is conferred by the Holy Spirit, however, not by man. The man is just the vessel who speaks it forth.

God's Guidance System

CORRECTIONAL PROPHECY

The third type of prophecy is correctional in nature. This word from God contains a correction, a rebuke or an exhortation. This is the type of prophecy many people have in mind when they think of the prophetic gifting; and this is what makes them afraid of prophets. As we have already noted, however, if this prophecy is truly from the Lord, it will be redemptive in nature, for the Lord does not break down without building up.

JUDGMENTAL PROPHECY

The final type of prophecy is a judgmental word. This is not judgementalism in a human, critical sense, but it carries with it the very judgment of God. Again, this is rare these days. We do see this type of prophecy at work, however, in the early Church:

> But a certain man named Ananias, with Sapphira his wife, sold a possession. And he kept back part of the proceeds, his wife also being aware of it, and brought a certain part and laid it at the apostles' feet.
> But Peter said, "Ananias, why has Satan filled your heart to lie to the Holy Spirit and keep back part of the price of the land for yourself? While it remained, was it not your own? And after it was sold, was it not in your own control? Why have you conceived this thing in your heart? You have not lied to men but to God."
> Then Ananias, hearing these words, fell down and breathed his last. So great fear came upon all those

who heard these things. And the young men arose and wrapped him up, carried him out, and buried him.

Now it was about three hours later when his wife came in, not knowing what had happened. And Peter answered her, "Tell me whether you sold the land for so much?"

She said, "Yes, for so much."

Then Peter said to her, "How is it that you have agreed together to test the Spirit of the Lord? Look, the feet of those who have buried your husband are at the door, and they will carry you out."

Then immediately she fell down at his feet and breathed her last. And the young men came in and found her dead, and carrying her out, buried her by her husband.   Acts 5:1-10

Why did Peter question this man and his wife? Was he trying to harass them? Of course not. He was giving them space for repentance. It soon became apparent, however, that there was no repentance on their part, and his message shifted to judgment. That judgment was swift. Before many minutes men were carrying the body of Ananias out the door, and his wife would soon follow. Their judgement had not come from any man, but from God.

MAKING ROOM FOR MISTAKES

If you want to have a perfect church, then don't have any members. It's the members who are imperfect. If you don't want to have any errors committed in ministry, then do away with the spiritual gifts being given to mortals. As long as the anointing of God is flowing through humans, mistakes will happen. By opening the door to people, we are opening the door to abuse, but we must take that risk.

Proverbs teaches:

Where no oxen are, the trough is clean; But much increase comes by the strength of an ox.

Proverbs 14:4

If we want to keep a clean trough, if we expect to maintain a tidy church, with everything always in order and where things flow neatly along well-ordered paths, then we must keep the oxen out. That won't work because we need them. As long as we allow spiritual gifts to flow, there will always be an occasional potential for wrong, an occasional showing of the fleshly nature, but the oxen — the gifts, the flowing in the Spirit — will produce results. Their strength will multiply your blessing and will prosper your spirit. They will bring forth what you need them to bring forth.

You will have to clean out the trough from time to time. Where there is life, things tend to get a bit messy. It is true in the spiritual as well as the natural. Only be diligent to keep the refuse separate from the reward.

This cleaning process is the role of those in authority. This is why we need church government. Someone has to see to it that the chores are done. Someone has to see to it that the trash is taken out. We cannot always prevent wrong from occurring, but as pastors, we can clean it up, and, by the grace of God, keep it from harming anyone. It's called damage control. We must be willing to keep the stall clean — if we are to see a plentiful harvest.

SEEK OTHER WITNESSES

In relationship to prophecy, learn practical discernment. Learn to eat the fish and spit out the bones. If you fail to do this, you will become fearful of the prophetic gift, will be afraid to operate in it yourself, and will be afraid to receive a word of prophecy from others. This is why we must *"hold fast that which is good"* after we have tested everything and let the rest go.

If you live in an area or attend a church where prophecy is accepted and thrives, take care to seek additional confirmation to what God is saying. It seems all too easy for some to rely on this witness alone, partly because it seems to be the most glamorous witness, at least to those who measure spirituality by externals. For those who happen to be lazy, this can become the simplest method of guidance and reason to neglect their own personal spiritual growth. They are content enough just to coast along until someone brings them the next prophecy.

Don't be guilty of placing too much emphasis on any single principle while neglecting others. Life is just too complex to allow one witness to be our overriding source. That is why God has given us these seven.

Make sure that every prophecy is in line with the Sacred Scriptures. This is the reason that many prophets speak forth the written Word as part of their prophetic utterance. Let each of us examine our hearts and motives in either giving or receiving a word of prophecy, so that we might use well *God's Guidance System.*

CHAPTER 6

GODLY COUNSEL

I will bless the LORD who has given me counsel.
                                          Psalm 16:7

The fourth principle of *God's Guidance System* is godly counsel. This principle helps us to look beyond our own wisdom and to hear and apply the wisdom God has given to others. We can share such wisdom with each other because of Christ who is our *"Counselor"*:

> *For unto us a Child is born,*
> *Unto us a Son is given;*
> *And the government will be upon His shoulder.*
> *And His name will be called*
> *Wonderful, Counselor, Mighty God,*
> *Everlasting Father, Prince of Peace.*   Isaiah 9:6

Isaiah spoke further of the coming Lord Jesus:

> *There shall come forth a Rod from the stem of Jesse,*
> *And a Branch shall grow out of his roots.*

God's Guidance System

*The Spirit of the L*ORD *shall rest upon Him,*
The Spirit of wisdom and understanding,
The Spirit of counsel and might,
*The Spirit of knowledge and of the fear of the L*ORD.

Isaiah 11:1-2

There are seven manifestations of the Holy Spirit (who abode upon Christ) listed here, and one of them is *"the Spirit of counsel."* If the Holy Spirit was *"the Spirit of counsel"* and He made Jesus the *"Counselor,"* then we can expect that same *"Spirit of counsel"* to be at work in the Church today. The Holy Spirit who came upon Jesus is the same Holy Spirit who comes upon God's people today, therefore the same *"Spirit of counsel"* dwells in us.

Most of us have, at one time or another, received godly counsel that made a real difference in our lives. That godly counsel or godly advice may have come from an authority figure, from an adviser or from a friend. It may have come to us through some formal counselling session, or it may have come about very naturally in the course of our daily exchanges with one anther. It may have come when we were specifically seeking advice on some important decision we faced or it may have come about without our seeking it. Whatever the case, God can use those whose wisdom we trust to help us find His will.

If we are wise, we will heed the godly wisdom that comes our way. This, all too often, is not the case. In the present climate of self-will in the world around us, far too many Christians are slow to hear the wise counsel of others around them and often have to learn everything the hard way. What a tragedy this is!

Godly Counsel

Why is it so hard for us to believe that someone else may be wiser than we are? Sometimes we are just too busy talking about our own ideas and plans to be able to hear what others are trying to tell us. We want the spotlight to be on us. We want others to see how spiritual we are. In this way, we sometimes miss out on what God wants to say to us through another person.

Receiving wise counsel requires listening, and you can't talk and listen at the same time.

There is a time for talking and, once we have listened and had a chance to let the Holy Spirit speak to us about the counsel we have received, maybe then we can talk. But if we don't learn to listen first, we are doomed to miss many great things from God.

Proverbs teaches:

> *Where there is no counsel, the people fall;*
> *But in the multitude of counselors there is safety.*
>
> Proverbs 11:14

> *For by wise counsel you will wage your own war,*
> *And in a multitude of counselors there is safety.*
>
> Proverbs 24:6

Anytime we have a major decision to make, we must seek godly counsel. We should not be satisfied just to hear the opinion of a single person, but should seek the security, the *"safety,"* of *"a multitude of counselors."* Why is this? So that we can receive a variety of viewpoints. Different people have different ways of looking at things and will give counsel accordingly. Hearing from more people can give us a clearer and, perhaps, more complete picture of what God is saying.

God's Guidance System

A SECOND OPINION

If your doctor told you that you needed to have major surgery, you would be well advised to get a second opinion. That is not offensive to your doctor. It is just the logical thing to do. If your life is threatened, you want the best medical advice possible.

The second expert you consult may well give the same advice as the first, but he may also offer some new insight that will be helpful. Whatever the case, once you have gotten a second opinion, you can rest more assured that you are receiving the best possible care.

If we are willing to follow this guideline concerning our physical well-being, why are we not willing to do the same concerning our spiritual lives? There is so much at stake here. When we speak of our health, we know that our very life is at stake, and when we speak of our spiritual welfare, we should realize that our very purpose in life, our destiny, our future, and the will of God for us all hangs in the balance.

Receiving godly counsel requires that we walk in humility. We cannot receive from another person if we think we know more than he does, or if we believe our experience is more far-reaching than his. We must be willing to lay such thoughts aside and to listen to what the Lord would say through someone else.

KING DAVID SOUGHT COUNSEL

King David had full authority to reign over Israel. He was not required to listen to anyone. He had the power to make every decision. The choices he made alone, however, without seeking counsel from others, only brought him trouble, and he lived to regret them.

When he saw Bathsheba bathing on the rooftop, David did not call any of his counselors to ask if it was wise for a king to enter into an illicit relationship with another man's wife. When Bathsheba became pregnant while her husband was away at war, David did not call any of his counselors to ask if it was wise for him to have the man, Uriah, one of his trusted military leaders, killed. When David was advised against conducting a census to number the men of fighting age in his kingdom, but he ignored that counsel and went ahead with the numbering, God judged him for it and the result was that many innocent people died. Bad decisions have serious consequences.

David also made many good decisions and, for these, he sought and received wise counsel from his trusted advisors. He wisely surrounded himself with people of wisdom, among them:

> *Of the sons of Issachar who had understanding of the times, to know what Israel ought to do, their chiefs were two hundred; and all their brethren were at their command.* 1 Chronicles 12:32

> *Also Jehonathan, David's uncle, was a counselor, a wise man, and a scribe; and Jehiel the son of Hachmoni was with the king's sons. Ahithophel was the king's counselor, and Hushai the Archite was the king's companion. After Ahithophel was Jehoiada the son of Benaiah, then Abiathar. And the general of the king's army was Joab.* 1 Chronicles 27:32-34

David surrounded himself with men who were attuned to the times, men whom he trusted and to whom he could turn at any moment for guidance. For the most part, therefore, he is remembered as a wise king. He understood the value of godly counsel. When he got it, he did well, and when he didn't, he suffered.

David was wise enough to know that he didn't know everything. That is exactly what we must confess to ourselves every day. It is only too true. We *don't* know everything. We are all in the process of learning.

I have been in the ministry for many years, but I don't know everything yet. I am still forced to talk with others in ministry, and some of those I seek for counsel are younger than I am — both in years and experience. I recognize, however, the gift of God and the wisdom of God in their lives, and I call upon their expertise when I have need.

I can't afford to say, "Let them call me. I'm the man of experience, wisdom and knowledge around here. I've been in the ministry for over thirty years." That would be a sure formula for getting into trouble. We must walk in humility before one another, respecting both the person and the gift of God within other individuals.

REHOBOAM'S FOLLY

We can see many examples in scripture of people who were proud and who believed that they did indeed know it all. David's grandson, the proud Rehoboam, was just such a person. He was not wise enough to receive counsel. Before they made him king, the people of Israel posed a question to him:

Godly Counsel

*Then they sent for him and called him. And Jeroboam
and all Israel came and spoke to Rehoboam, saying,
"Your father made our yoke heavy; now therefore,
lighten the burdensome service of your father and his
heavy yoke which he put on us, and we will serve you."
So he said to them, "Come back to me after three days."
And the people departed.
Then King Rehoboam consulted the elders who stood
before his father Solomon while he still lived, saying,
"How do you advise me to answer these people?"
And they spoke to him, saying, "If you are kind to
these people, and please them, and speak good words
to them, they will be your servants forever."*

2 Chronicles 10:3-7

The men whom Rehoboam consulted were wise and
gave him sound counsel. They were some of the same
men who had surrounded King Solomon, the wisest man
who ever lived. Even he had needed counselors.

These men were saying to Rehoboam, the would-be
king, "Your father asked the people to bear too much,
and as a consequence, there was rebellion. You now have
a chance to make things right with the people and to
heal those old wounds. If you will do this, they will
gladly serve you."

This counsel did not seem very wise to Rehoboam.
He was a rash young man, and had perhaps already
made up his mind about what he intended to do. He,
therefore, ignored the counsel of the wise and tested elders and consulted, instead, with those who had no right
to be giving him advice:

Then the young men who had grown up with him spoke to him, saying, "Thus you should speak to the people who have spoken to you, saying, 'Your father made our yoke heavy, but you make it lighter on us'; thus you shall say to them: 'My little finger shall be thicker than my father's waist! And now, whereas my father put a heavy yoke on you, I will add to your yoke; my father chastised you with whips, but I will chastise you with scourges!' "

So Jeroboam and all the people came to Rehoboam on the third day, as the king had directed, saying, "Come back to me the third day." Then the king answered them roughly. King Rehoboam rejected the advice of the elders.   2 Chronicles 10:10-13

These young men told Rehoboam exactly what he wanted to hear. He was just like them and no doubt believed that by taking the action they suggested he could secure an even stronger position than his beloved father and grandfather. He was wrong. When he refused to accept wise counsel, he split the kingdom into two parts and was able to rule over only a portion of the nation his father and grandfather had served so nobly.

Beloved, if the only counsel we seek is from people who are ambitious, immature and carnal, we are setting ourselves up for disaster. On the other hand, if we seek wise and godly counsel from those who are qualified to give it to us, yet we refuse to heed that counsel, then we have rejected *God's Guidance System* in favor of our own. This, again, is a recipe for disaster.

Rehoboam failed on both counts, and disaster followed. Not only was his kingdom divided, but it was also shortly invaded by the Egyptians:

> *And it happened in the fifth year of King Rehoboam, that Shishak king of Egypt came up against Jerusalem, because they had transgressed against the LORD. Then Shemaiah the prophet came to Rehoboam and the leaders of Judah, who were gathered together in Jerusalem because of Shishak, and said to them, "Thus says the LORD: 'You have forsaken Me, and therefore I also have left you in the hand of Shishak.'"*
> *So Shishak king of Egypt came up against Jerusalem, and took away the treasures of the house of the LORD and the treasures of the king's house; he took everything. He also carried away the gold shields which Solomon had made.* 2 Chronicles 12:2, 5 and 9

God allowed Shishak, king of Egypt, to strip the house of God of all of its treasures. What does this mean? In the Scriptures, Egypt is the type or representation of the world's system. Those treasures that were stolen by Egypt represent the gifts of God in the Church. Rehoboam's refusal to receive godly counsel finally caused the loss of the treasures of the house of God as the world's system came in and took over. Rehoboam was left to make bronze replicas of the golden shields David had made. The bronze of judgment was replacing the gold of the nature and divinity of God.

If you want the gifts of God to operate effectively in your life, then you must learn to receive wise and godly counsel. Rehoboam was not a wise man, but hopefully we can learn from his bad example.

God's Guidance System

TOO PROUD TO SEEK COUNSEL

One of the main reasons we fail to seek counsel from others is that we are too proud. We don't want people to know that we have a problem and that we need help. We want to be seen as invincible, wise and spiritual. Consequently we cut ourselves off from those who could help us along the way. This is dangerous:

> *A man who isolates himself seeks his own desire;*
> *He rages against all wise judgment.*
> *A fool has no delight in understanding,*
> *But in expressing his own heart.*   Proverbs 18:1-2

We need one another, and we need to be open and honest enough to seek counsel. To do otherwise is to be isolated, cutting ourselves off from wisdom.

SEEKING COUNSEL FROM THE WRONG PEOPLE

We must be careful whom we go to for counsel. Just because a person is a friend doesn't always make him wise or godly, and the counsel of such a person might lead us astray.

One good rule is never to go to someone for advice when they need more help than you do. Don't seek spiritual advice from someone who is not close to God. If a person is lukewarm in his love for God or is not attuned to the Holy Spirit, he is not someone you should be trusting for counsel.

Why ask a person who has been married half a dozen times how to have a good marriage? I'm not saying something against that individual. I am saying that he cannot possibly help you. That's all. The marriage he has right now may be great, and it may last, but his past failures in this regard eliminate him from contention as a wise counselor worthy of our attention.

Like Rehoboam, many of us have the wrong type of influences in their lives. Paul warned the Corinthian believers:

> *Do not be deceived: "Evil company corrupts good habits."*   1 Corinthians 15:33

Who are the people you spend time with? What are they like? If you spend time with those who are bitter, those who have their own agendas, those who are critical or are gossips, their sinful attitudes will corrupt you like a cancer corrupts the good cells in a natural body. Before you realize it, you will have caught the same spirit they have, and you will have begun to think and act in the same manner. You will waste your life by listening to the ungodly counsel of such people. Don't just walk away from them; run.

Many young people develop wrong attitudes and wrong lifestyles because they get advice on dating, home, parents, school and the future from their friends — friends who are often more confused than they are. If young people are not getting advice from their friends, they're getting it from television, and we all know what terrible values the average television program puts forth today. No wonder young people have so many problems! Often, however, it is because they are not really looking for wise counsel. They just want someone who will agree with them.

Sadder yet is the fact that many parents today do not take their rightful place in giving wise counsel to their children. They want their children to develop their own ideals. They want perfect, quiet children who never make mistakes, but they are too busy living their own lives to really notice what their children are doing.

If parents have not received godly counsel themselves, they also don't have it to give. Many live a double standard before their children and, therefore, the children have no confidence in their parent's words. Far too many parents have tried to teach one thing and live another. And children are not stupid. They see that their parents' words and actions in public do not agree with the reality of their private life. Children, therefore, are learning that it is okay to be phony, to be truth twisters, to be pretenders.

Research tells us that the family still has the greatest influence on children — more than anyone or anything else. Oh that parents would take the time to use their influence wisely! There is still hope for present generations, but we must give ourselves to our children and allow them to see us giving ourselves to God.

EARLY BIBLICAL EXAMPLES OF GODLY COUNSEL

One of the earliest biblical mentions of someone receiving godly counsel from another person is found in the book of Exodus. Moses was counseled by his father-in-law, Jethro:

> *And so it was, on the next day, that Moses sat to judge the people; and the people stood before Moses from morning until evening.*

Godly Counsel

So when Moses' father-in-law saw all that he did for the people, he said, "What is this thing that you are doing for the people? Why do you alone sit, and all the people stand before you from morning until evening?"

And Moses said to his father-in-law, "Because the people come to me to inquire of God. When they have a difficulty, they come to me, and I judge between one and another; and I make known the statutes of God and His laws."

So Moses' father-in-law said to him, "The thing that you do is not good. Both you and these people who are with you will surely wear yourselves out. For this thing is too much for you; you are not able to perform it by yourself. Listen now to my voice; I will give you counsel, and God will be with you."

Exodus 18:13-19

Jethro was able to be objective about Moses' style of leadership, and he saw something that he knew could prove fatal to his son-in-law and, therefore, to the nation as a whole. He said to Moses, *"The thing that you do is not good."* That is not what we like to hear, but we need to hear it sometimes. Our flesh never welcomes such words, but we need them nevertheless.

This would have been a golden opportunity for Moses to put his father-in-law in his place. He could have said, "Listen, Dad, how would you know what is best for these people? Did *you* lead them out from Egypt? Have *you* guided them as they journeyed? I think I'm the leader around here, and I resent you getting involved in my business! Let me do things my way." Fortunately, however, Moses was a man of humility and did not think too highly of himself than he should. He listened intently to Jethro's advice that he mentor other leaders and saw the wisdom of it. If he could prepare other leaders, the heavy load could be shared, and surely much more could be accomplished. Why hadn't he thought of that himself? he must have wondered.

Each of us has some Jethros whom God has allowed to be part of our lives, whether we know it or not and whether we like it or not. We must learn to listen to what these people have to say to us. True leaders and godly counselors, whether we realize it or not, have our best interests at heart. They are not trying to see who they can confuse and disorient. The voice of godly counsel is present for our benefit.

WHO IS COUNSELING YOU?

Who is counseling you? Some people say, "I'm not going to listen to anyone but God." That's fine, but perhaps He is trying to speak to you through your pastor, your leaders, your wife, your husband, and your spiritual brothers and sisters. Have you listened to what they are saying? If you insist on waiting for a voice from Heaven to supernaturally speak to you (with the accompanying lightning and thunder), you may wait for a very long time. God's voice is speaking to you all the time. Find someone that you trust and listen to their counsel, for in hearing them, you are hearing God.

Some of us can't receive counsel from others. We puff up and run out the door, offended in our spirits. When that is true, we can know that we are not yet wise people.

Godly Counsel

If we refuse to be examined because we are afraid we will be told that we are wrong, that indicates that our flesh is far too active still.

FAR FROM PERFECT

It's nice to be proven right, but I, for one, am also willing to be told that I am wrong sometimes. Try as we might, we are all far from perfect. Sometimes the Lord has to show us just how imperfect we are.

Once I prayed, "Lord, I so thank You that You have delivered me from anger." We were having a church picnic that day, and I loaded up my vehicle early and drove to the picnic site to help set up. As I drove into the place, I saw a sign that said very clearly, "No unloading in the pavilion area!" I was sure that didn't apply to me since I would be in and out very quickly, so I pulled in past the sign, got as close as I could to the pavilion and started to unload the car.

Suddenly, the park's caretaker appeared and began pointing out to me that my car should not be where it was. I couldn't believe he would be so petty. Didn't he know that I was the pastor? The whole thing upset me so that I slammed the door of the truck, jumped in and hit the accelerator as hard as I could. The truck went fishtailing out of the area as I kicked up a storm of grass and gravel and dirt. My wife was very embarrassed for me, and I was embarrassed too. God was just making me look in the mirror and see that I was not nearly as perfect as I had imagined.

If any of us gets to the place that we feel we are so perfect we don't need advice from anyone else, that person has a serious problem with pride. That's very dangerous, for God resists the proud and, as we have said, if God is resisting you, He certainly cannot be guiding you. Those who take this attitude, are going *"backward and not forward"*:

> But this is what I commanded them, saying, "Obey My voice, and I will be your God, and you shall be My people. And walk in all the ways that I have commanded you, that it may be well with you." Yet they did not obey or incline their ear, but followed the counsels and the dictates of their evil hearts, and went backward and not forward.   Jeremiah 7:23-24

Godly counsel exposes deception or blind spots in our lives and helps us move forward. Ungodly counsel brings us into further deception and sends us backwards. The Psalmist declared:

> Blessed is the man
> Who walks not in the counsel of the ungodly,
> Nor stands in the path of sinners,
> Nor sits in the seat of the scornful;
> But his delight is in the law of the LORD.
>   Psalm 1:1-2

THE COUNSEL OF OTHERS PROVIDES A MIRROR

Even though we have two eyes, we cannot see the back of our heads. The only way you can do that is to use a mirror, and godly counsel is just such a mirror. When someone gives you advice, they are not just picking on you. They're trying to help you. They see a problem that you can't see. They see something about you that you can't see for yourself.

None of us is very honest when it comes to evaluating ourselves. Our flesh doesn't want to believe anything bad about itself. We like to think we are fine just as we are, but God is continually calling us higher. We should be grateful to those whom God uses to show us a higher way. Why is it that we usually resent them instead?

When someone who is completely honest and loves God and loves you comes along and points out something in your life that can be improved, be happy about it. Thank them, and thank God.

Your "friends" may agree with your flesh that you are perfect and have no need of change. "Friends" often lie to maintain the "friendship." Be open to the truth for once.

Instead of resisting the godly advice of others, embrace it and ask God to help you change. If He has shown you an area where you need to change it's because He wants to help you make that change.

If someone comes along who can see into my blindspots, why should I not be grateful to them? I need that help. I rejoice in it:

> *The way of a fool is right in his own eyes, But he who heeds counsel is wise.*   Proverbs 12:15

We all know that you can't tell a fool anything, and since we don't want to be fools ourselves, we must learn to receive godly counsel.

God's Guidance System

OBEYING WHAT GOD SHOWS US THROUGH OTHERS

Often, when we are stressed and anxious, in tears and in emotional pain, we say, "I just don't know what to do!" I believe, however, that many times we do know what to do and are not willing to do it. God has made His will plain to us through those around us, but we refuse to recognize the wisdom of their words and embrace them. The moment we say yes to God, the pain eases, the grief is gone, and everything is fine.

Far too often in recent years the Christian world has been rocked by scandals of ministers and ministries falling. It doesn't happen overnight. Ministers or ministries fall because either they fail to seek wise counsel or they reject the wise counsel that God has already provided them. When we see them crash and burn it is only after a long process of neglect in this area of their lives.

If we hope to be around for "the long haul," we must have an attitude adjustment. Our many talents won't keep us. Only wise counsel from God's servants will. We are admonished:

> *Let us search out and examine our ways,*
> *And turn back to the* LORD.   Lamentations 3:40

CHANGE IS NEEDED

The Lord provides godly counsel for us so that we can produce righteousness and godliness. These are the natural fruit of responding to the guidance of the Lord. Some people are convinced that they can change their lives by changing their marriage partner, by changing their job, their place of residence or the church they attend. But none of these will produce the necessary change because you will still be you. Wherever you move, you are still taking yourself along, and you are the problem — not the location, not the partner, not the job. If you refuse to change, you will go on hurting more and more people and bringing more and more destruction upon your own life.

Isaiah prophesied:

> *Therefore the Lord says,*
> *The LORD of hosts, the Mighty One of Israel,*
> *"Ah, I will rid Myself of My adversaries,*
> *And take vengeance on My enemies.*
> *I will turn My hand against you,*
> *And thoroughly purge away your dross,*
> *And take away all your alloy.*
> *I will restore your judges as at the first,*
> *And your counselors as at the beginning.*
> *Afterward you shall be called the city of righteousness, the faithful city."*   Isaiah 1:24-26

When we receive and heed the guidance and wisdom God gives us through godly counselors, we can become *"the city of righteousness, the faithful city"* that God desires to establish on the Earth. Let us become God's Zion to the world around us by heeding *God's Guidance System.* Don't be foolish. Receive godly counsel and grow in righteousness.

CHAPTER 7

CIRCUMSTANCES

For we walk by faith, not by sight.

2 Corinthians 5:7

Circumstantial confirmation to the will of God can be the most misunderstood element of *God's Guidance System*, and because of this, I always urge people not to ever let circumstances alone be the determining factor as they are being led by God. Especially when it comes to major decisions, it is very dangerous to be led by circumstances. God can and does use circumstances to help guide us, but we must use wisdom in interpreting what we see happening around us, for Satan also influences our circumstances.

The word circumstance is made up of two root words: *circum*, which means "around," and *stance*, which means "in position." So circumstances are the things that are occurring around your current position in life at any given moment. When we begin to look at circumstances, to see whether or not God is speaking to us through them, our hearts must be pure or we can make a mistake. It is also essential to be filled with the Spirit and to have spiritual discernment to understand this type of guidance.

THE CASE OF GIDEON

The case of Gideon is probably the most well known biblical example of someone using circumstance as a tool for guidance. Of him, we read:

> *So Gideon said to God, "If You will save Israel by my hand as You have said — look, I shall put a fleece of wool on the threshing floor; if there is dew on the fleece only, and it is dry on all the ground, then I shall know that You will save Israel by my hand, as You have said." And it was so. When he rose early the next morning and squeezed the fleece together, he wrung the dew out of the fleece, a bowlful of water.*
> *Then Gideon said to God, "Do not be angry with me, but let me speak just once more: Let me test, I pray, just once more with the fleece; let it now be dry only on the fleece, but on all the ground let there be dew." And God did so that night. It was dry on the fleece only, but there was dew on all the ground.*
>
> Judges 6:36-40

Gideon thus used circumstances as a method of guidance.

Many Christians have tried this method and failed, and we need to see why that is. They say: if such and such a thing happens, then I will know that God is telling me to do this or that. I believe the first error these people are making is to greatly simplify Gideon's story. There was more to it than that.

God had already told Gideon to go to war and had already promised that Gideon would be victorious. Gideon was not looking for a new direction, but rather for a confirmation for guidance he had already received in another form. Before he looked for the sign, he asked God about it. He did not simply say, "Well, if this happens, I'll believe it's God." He did not go to the Lord in presumption, ordering God belligerently, "God, if this is You, then You had better do this or else I won't obey!" He went to God in humility, specifically asking for this confirmation, and God responded graciously to him, using the circumstances of Gideon's life to bring about His purpose.

THE STRANGE CASE OF BALAAM

Another interesting case is found in the book of Numbers. The people of Israel, still wandering in the wilderness, had encamped on the plains of Moab. The Moabites had seen what God had done for His people, and they were afraid of the Israelites. Balak, the king of Moab, sent men to bring the prophet Balaam to him. He understood Balaam to be a man who knew how to bless or curse, and he wanted him to curse the Israelites.

The men sent by Balak came to Balaam and gave him the king's message. Balaam invited them to spend the night at his house while he sought the Lord as to whether or not he should go with them. God answered him:

God's Guidance System

*And God said to Balaam, "You shall not go with them;
you shall not curse the people, for they are blessed."*

Numbers 22:12

God's response to Balaam's prayer was not difficult
to understand. He left nothing open to interpretation.
Balaam was not to go with these men, and he was not to
curse the people of Israel, *"for they [were] blessed."* So Balaam declined to accompany the men sent for him.

This was not an easy decision to make. How would
you feel if a king sent his leaders as messengers to bring
you to help him? Balaam's assistance was being sought
by a great and powerful man. That idea would have ap-
pealed to most of us. After all, God has called us to
prophesy to the nations and to come before kings and
has promised that our gift will make room for us and
that we will be exalted before men. This seemed like a
wonderful opportunity.

This is what is so difficult about discerning when circumstances do and do not cause us to respond. Satan
knows how to place pleasant-looking circumstances before us too. Balaam was wise enough not to jump at what
looked like a good thing, but to pray first and seek the
Lord. The word he received from God guided him, not
the prevailing circumstances.

When Balak received word that Balaam had declined
his invitation, he was disappointed, but he was not ready
to give up yet. He sent more leaders, *"more numerous
and more honorable"* than the first (verse 15). Their request
was the same. Now Balaam was really drawn by the circumstances. How often does a king ask for a favor —

twice? Again, however, Balaam displayed his wisdom by asking the men to stay overnight so that he could seek the mind of God in the matter.

God's response to Balaam's first inquiry had been unequivocal: don't go and don't curse the Israelites. There really didn't seem to be much of a chance that God would change His mind — no matter how much of a reward Balaam had been promised for going. But something had changed this time. Perhaps because of the lure of serving a king or the lure of the reward or the pride of doing something so important or being sought by such an important man, or because of all these reasons, Balaam's focus had now shifted. He was now looking more at the prevailing circumstances than he was at God.

The first answer had been so clear that Balaam should never have sought a second. He knew God's will in this matter. Because the circumstances seemed so ideal, however, Balaam went back to God a second time. This time, God allowed Balaam to go, but He was angry that he had asked again. He already knew Balaam's decision. The prophet wanted to do this thing — whatever God thought about it. Sometimes God allows us to go our own way simply because we are so set on doing it anyway.

We might submit to God's will in such cases, but we do it quite grudgingly. Many times He allows us to have our own way in these cases, just to teach us a lesson. He allows us to face some trouble so that the next time we will think twice before insisting on doing things our own way. When we insist on going our own way, God has a way of showing us who is in charge:

So Balaam rose in the morning, saddled his donkey, and went with the princes of Moab. Then God's anger was aroused because he went, and the Angel of the LORD took His stand in the way as an adversary against him. And he was riding on his donkey, and his two servants were with him. Now the donkey saw the Angel of the LORD standing in the way with His drawn sword in His hand, and the donkey turned aside out of the way and went into the field. So Balaam struck the donkey to turn her back onto the road.

Numbers 22:21-23

Balaam struck the poor donkey three times, until an amazing thing happened:

Then the LORD opened the mouth of the donkey, and she said to Balaam, "What have I done to you, that you have struck me these three times?"
And Balaam said to the donkey, "Because you have abused me. I wish there were a sword in my hand, for now I would kill you!"
So the donkey said to Balaam, "Am I not your donkey on which you have ridden, ever since I became yours, to this day? Was I ever disposed to do this to you?"
And he said, "No."
Then the LORD opened Balaam's eyes, and he saw the Angel of the LORD standing in the way with His drawn sword in His hand; and he bowed his head and fell flat on his face. And the Angel of the LORD said to him, "Why have you struck your donkey these three times? Behold, I have come out to stand against you, because your way is perverse before Me. The donkey

126

saw Me and turned aside from Me these three times.
If she had not turned aside from Me, surely I would
also have killed you by now, and let her live."
And Balaam said to the Angel of the LORD, "I have
sinned, for I did not know You stood in the way
against me. Now therefore, if it displeases You, I will
turn back."   Numbers 22:28-34

"I have sinned." Balaam had been so wrapped up in the circumstances of his royal invitation that he had not been able to see what was right in front of him in the spirit realm. If we are to be guided by circumstances, we must be absolutely sure that we maintain our eyes open to the things of the Spirit as well.

Too many Christians judge God's will by circumstance alone. When they are in some sort of a bind and suddenly the phone rings or someone knocks on the door offering something that looks like it might be a way out, they immediately grasp that "opportunity." They declare, "This must be God's will, for it came looking for me. I didn't go looking for it."

This may come as a revelation to some, but the devil knows our address just as well as God does. We must learn to use discernment when evaluating circumstances, and we must line up some more witnesses before we can move forward. We cannot afford to make major decisions based on circumstances alone. If we fail to carefully examine circumstances and accept them immediately as from God, we may end up far off course. And we can easily lose our sense of destiny when our movements are dictated by what is going on around us.

God's Guidance System

GOOD? OR BAD?

Good news/bad news stories are very popular these days. Here's an interesting one:

THE FIRST MAN: "I went flying in an airplane."
THE SECOND MAN: "That's good!"
THE FIRST MAN: "Well, not exactly; the engine quit."
THE SECOND MAN: "That's bad!"
THE FIRST MAN: "Yes, but I jumped out with a parachute."
THE SECOND MAN: "That's good!"
THE FIRST MAN: "Well ... the parachute didn't open."
THE SECOND MAN: "That's bad!"
THE FIRST MAN: "Yes, but there was a haystack beneath me."
THE SECOND MAN: "That's good!"
THE FIRST MAN: "But there was a pitchfork in the haystack."

It's a silly story, but for all too many Christians, it has become reality. They go from moment to moment, constantly judging their circumstances. One minute everything seems to be going well, and the next minute, everything seems to be going bad.

The problem is that we never have the whole story. Where you are today is not necessarily where you will be tomorrow. Sometimes the circumstances are speaking to you, but God wants you to speak to the circumstances. You must live close enough to God to discern which it is to be for the moment.

Circumstances

HOW CIRCUMSTANCES SOMETIMES HELP US

Balaam's donkey was a type or a representation of our circumstances. Balaam was riding along on his circumstances when suddenly things started to go wrong. He wanted to go on because he had an important appointment to keep, but his circumstances were not cooperating.

What should Balaam have done in this situation? He did exactly what most of us do. He began to attack his circumstances.

And how did Balaam's circumstances respond to this abuse? First, they took Balaam off the road and into the field, and next they began to crush his foot against a wall. Finally, circumstances simply lay down with him and on him.

That which was visible was being influenced by that which was invisible; the natural was being affected by the spiritual. We judge most situations by what we can see, but we fail to see what is happening in the unseen world around us. God sees, and God knows, and our circumstances are often the work of His grace.

The unseen for Balaam was the angel that had been sent by God to oppose the prophet's journey. Balaam was a man of God, but his mind was so taken with other thoughts that he could not see the angel. The donkey, however, did see the angel and responded to him.

Sometimes we are so blinded by our own will that we cannot see that God is not in the mixture. He is then forced to allow circumstances to oppose us, to keep us from doing what He knows will only hurt or destroy us.

Often, when things are going wrong around us, it is

because we are out of the will of God, and, just like Balaam, we haven't been able to see it.

All that Balaam knew was that circumstances were turning against him, but he didn't know why. So he became angry with his circumstances, just like we often do. Some of us grow so angry at the circumstances life has dealt us that we rail against them, trying to beat them into line with what we think is God's will for us at the moment. When this happens, we need to take a second look, to observe more carefully what is happening and why. We may find that we have been raving against the very thing that God has sent to save us from ourselves.

SEEMING FAILURES, IN REALITY, MAY BE SUCCESSES

That broken engagement: How utterly humiliating! *What am I going to do?* you wonder. *I was sure that she was the right one for me. Now I am confused and don't know what direction to take next.*

Perhaps all is not lost. I can still resolve this impasse. I will go to her and apologize on my knees. I'll send flowers. I'll send the Philharmonic Orchestra if I have to. I'll do whatever it takes!

If this is your case, I would say to you: Leave this situation alone for the moment until you can see more clearly what is at work here. God may be saving you from a lot of future heartache.

That new job you wanted ... You thought that if you could get it, everything would work better for you. You prayed and you believed, and you were sure that you were going to be hired. When someone in the company came to you and said, "I saw your application lying on the boss's desk, and I think you've got the job," you were so sure it was a done deal that you began to get ready for your new position. You were already thinking about how you would spend the extra money. You reworked your entire budget to match your new salary.

Then you got that terrible phone call. You were sure it was good news and you ran to answer the phone. But then you heard those words, "This is Sam from the Employee Department calling to let you know that we're very sorry, but your application has been denied. We appreciate the effort you put forth to apply and we hope that there might be something for you in the future."

You were devastated by this news. How could this happen to you? Did you say something wrong? Did you dress wrong the day of the interview? Should you have been willing to work for less? And what should you do now?

If that sounds familiar, it may be time for you to let go of the whole matter. It may have been God using circumstances to keep you from taking that job or working for that company. If so, it means that He has something better for you that you don't yet know about.

That dead battery on your car ... It altered your schedule and messed up your day and you were so upset that you kicked the car, just like Balaam beating his donkey. You were able to deal with the problem quickly, but you were not at all happy about it. You kept muttering, "I'm going to be late! I'll never make it on time now!"

Finally, when you were on your way again and trying to make up the lost time, you suddenly saw up ahead a police car waving for traffic to slow down.

"What's going on?" you asked the officer.

God's Guidance System

"There was a tragic accident up here about a half an hour ago," he answered. "Several people were killed and many others were injured. You'll have to take this exit off the freeway until the wreck can be cleared from the road."

When you think about it, you realize that if you had not experienced a failed battery, you would have been there at just the time the accident occurred. God was saving your life and all you could do was mutter and kick the car. These type of things happen much more often than we realize.

Expect God's Surprises

Once, when Viv and I were flying to New Orleans from Honolulu, we had paid for our tickets to be delivered to the airport. We got to the airport and stood in line for what seemed like forever and, when we finally got to the head of the line at the check-in desk, we were told that our tickets had not yet arrived. This was distressing because we had a car waiting for us in New Orleans.

After a long discussion, the airlines issued us tickets there on the spot, but the ticket agent mistakenly typed in a different flight number for the portion of the flight from St. Louis to New Orleans. We didn't notice this until we tried to board that flight later the same day. "I'm sorry," the agent said, "but you're not booked on this flight. You're scheduled to leave on our next flight."

That next flight was not scheduled to leave for more than four hours, so we tried to argue with the lady. We showed her our baggage claim ticket which plainly stated that we were supposed to be leaving on the first flight. We showed our typed itinerary which confirmed that schedule.

"I'm sorry," she said, "this plane is full. Someone at the airport in Honolulu has made a mistake on your ticket and typed in the other flight number, and there is nothing I can do."

"But, Ma'am," I insisted, "you don't understand. We've got to be there!"

She said, "I'm really sorry. There's really nothing we can do. If you want to sit here nearby and wait until everyone boards to see if there is a chance for standby, you can. That's all I can offer."

I was getting very upset about that time and I might have raised more of a fuss about it, but, fortunately, Viv was more levelheaded. She reached over and took my arm and said, "Come on. Let's go and sit down."

We sat down to wait, but inwardly I was fuming. *This really burns me up. Why do people have to be so incompetent? Don't they understand all the hardship this will cause us by arriving late in New Orleans? And what will we do around here for the next four hours? Isn't this lovely?*

We had been sitting there no more than five or ten minutes, however, when an agent approached us. She bent down so that what she said could not be heard by others. "Here are two first-class boarding passes," she whispered. "Please don't tell anybody else. We're sorry for the inconvenience. Have a nice flight to New Orleans."

About that time, I felt about as big as a grasshopper. What would have happened, I wondered, if I had let my anger erupt like I wanted to? We would not have been allowed in the baggage compartment, let alone first class. God had been at work in my circumstances, and I had been too distracted to realize it. He had a wonderful surprise for us. We were flying to New Orleans first class.

We live our lives looking forward, but we understand our lives looking backward. We are often heard to say such things as:

> *"Thank God, I didn't marry him."*
> *"Thank God, I didn't get hooked up with her."*
> *"Thank God I wasn't able to come up with the money to invest in that venture."*
> *"Thank God I couldn't afford that at the time."*

We cannot see the end from the beginning, but God knows.

God's Rights vs. Your Rights

When you gave yourself to Jesus, you did just that. He has the right to order your life, and He doesn't have to ask your permission to do it. If you persist in going against His will, as Balaam did, He will allow you to do it, for He honors your free will, but you will surely pay the consequences.

Balaam was on his way to do something that God did not want him to do, and God had every right to stand in the prophet's way. He gave Balaam permission to go, but He was angry with him because he went.

This is an insight into the mind and the heart of God. God looks at our hearts and will sometimes give us what we want — despite the fact that it is not good for us or that it is not His perfect will for us. He lets us have something until we are sick of it and realize why He didn't want us to have it in the first place. His ways are always better.

When we insist on doing things our own way, the result can be *"leanness [of] soul"*:

> *They soon forgot His works;*
> *They did not wait for His counsel,*
> *But lusted exceedingly in the wilderness,*
> *And tested God in the desert.*
> *And He gave them their request,*
> *But sent leanness into their soul.*   Psalm 106:13-15

What was happening here? The people of Israel were crying out for something that God did not want them to have (and when we say that God does not want us to have something, it means that He has something better for us). In the case of the Israelites, God had given them manna miraculously from Heaven, and they were thankful for it — at first. Soon, however, they grew tired of eating manna in the morning, manna at lunch time and manna for supper, and began to think again about Egypt and to desire the foods they had grown accustomed to eating there.

The manna was nourishing, and through it God was sustaining a multitude of people in the wilderness, for He is the Bread of life. But they wanted meat. "Give us flesh!" they cried. "We want flesh!"

God said, "All right! I will give you what you want. I don't want to do it, but I will." He then caused a strong wind to begin to blow, and it blew quails into the camp.

The people got very excited. "Look," they shouted. "Just what we wanted. God has given us meat." And so they had fried quail, baked quail, boiled quail and stewed quail ... until finally they began to say, "We're sick of quail. Don't mention quail to us again. We hate quail!"

That's exactly what happens when we insist on doing things our own way. We cannot be blessed and satisfied when we deny God's will for our lives. This is more serious than just deciding what we are going to eat for supper. Until that time, the people of Israel had rejoiced in divine health. When they insisted on their own way, however, sickness and death came among them.

It is not known if perhaps some people had lagged behind on other portions of the journey and gotten sick or died because they got out from under the cloud of God's glory. It could well have happened. Otherwise, there had been no disease and no death among the great throng of people that moved on toward the Promised Land. Now it came.

For many of us, this may explain why certain things are happening to us, why our donkey refuses to move forward. God is placing roadblocks in our way so that we will not be destroyed. We just haven't realized it yet.

GOD USES PEOPLE AROUND US

Often, when God uses our circumstances, we think that people around us are the problem. *What a terrible boss I am saddled with! If I could only have a different boss, I am sure that I could do better. This man makes life so difficult for me.*

Circumstances

The problem is not your boss. God may be using your boss to resist what you are trying to do that would get you into trouble.

What about your spouse? What about that relative? What about that Christian brother or sister? It could be that what you think is a problem in one of them is really the hand of God trying to keep you from messing your life up completely. He can even use the IRS when He wants to speak to you. He is God. Don't limit Him.

If you have failed to listen to God, to an anointed pastor who is feeling the heart of God or even to the scriptural teachings, God may have to put some roadblocks in your way to keep you from destruction.

We blame so many things on the devil. "He's attacking us again. Anybody can see that." Maybe he is, but more than likely God has set an angel in the way to prevent you from doing yourself harm. The devil doesn't do nearly as much as we give him credit for. There is enough flesh in the church to sink us from within, without the devil's intervention.

The bad things that are happening to you may be God's way of warning you. If you refuse to heed those warnings, He will be forced to deal with you more severely, to do something that you cannot ignore. He doesn't like to do it, but He will do whatever is necessary. If need be, He will let you hear a donkey talk.

CIRCUMSTANCES CAN PROVE THAT YOU ARE IN THE RIGHT PLACE ... OR THE WRONG PLACE

God can use circumstances to confirm that you are in His will. Elijah was sent by God to a place of solitude.

The presence of the ravens who came and fed him daily proved to him that he was in the right place:

> *The ravens brought him bread and meat in the morning, and bread and meat in the evening; and he drank from the brook.* 1 Kings 17:6

CIRCUMSTANCES CAN ALSO PROVE THAT YOU ARE IN THE WRONG PLACE.

Jesus told of the prodigal son who came to himself only after he had landed in a pigsty. Until that moment, he had been having a wonderful time spending his inheritance, lavishing his father's hard-earned money on his "friends." Now that his money was gone his "friends" could not be found, and he soon realized just how terrible a mistake he had made. It was his circumstances, a pigpen, that brought him back to reality. If you wake up some morning in a pigpen, you might want to examine what got you there.

One thing is for certain: God never chooses for us to go to the pigpen. That is our choice. God allows it so that He can get us heading back home.

If you see God dealing with a backslider or a prodigal, don't be too quick to rescue them from the mess into which they have fallen. They may need to struggle through that hard place if they are to succeed. Sometimes we are too eager to help people out of their circumstances, when the circumstances are there for a purpose. We jump into a situation and try to snatch people out before God is through dealing with them. Later we wonder why these people we have helped end up back in the same type of situation again. Is it possible that they didn't have strength to go on because they didn't *work out [their] own salvation with fear and trembling"* (Philippians 2:12)? The circumstances God permits in our lives are for our growth, and we must work through them in order to succeed.

THE CASE OF PAUL

God used circumstances in Paul's life too. Once a fierce storm came up while he was being transported by ship to Rome. The ship was wrecked and all the cargo was lost, but none of the passengers were injured or killed, including Paul.

Why would God allow such a terrible thing to happen? He had a plan.

The mighty waves of the storm washed all the passengers up on the shores of Malta. The people of Malta had never heard the Gospel, and had circumstances been different, they would not have heard it that day either. But through what appeared to be a natural disaster, God gave Paul the opportunity to minister to the people of Malta and brought a great spiritual victory there.

The enemy always tries to thwart God's plan. Before Paul could preach the Gospel, the devil tried to kill him. As he was drying out around a fire, a poisonous viper came out of the burning sticks and bit him. Paul, however, suffered no harm from the bite. He simply shook the serpent off into the fire.

The locals were looking at Paul, expecting him to die at any moment. They knew how terribly potent the venom of that particular snake was. But Paul did not die. He didn't even get sick. It was this great miracle that opened the door to him to preach the Good News of Christ. Many people were healed in that place, and a church was established on the island.

What we consider to be a disaster can often become a great blessing. What we consider to be a detour may instead be a superhighway into the perfect will of God.

God doesn't have to ask our permission or give us any advance notice before He places a detour in our way. He may, but that's His decision.

I think that you can see that obtaining guidance in the middle of circumstances demands great maturity. It requires prayer, wisdom, and a lot of godly counsel to interpret circumstances. That is why we need the voice of two or three witnesses.

The Case of Joseph

What would have happened if Joseph had not been listening for God's voice when a whole series of terrible circumstances came his way? We can only imagine.

After many years had passed and he was installed as the Prime Minister of Egypt, his brothers came to purchase food. These were the men who had sold him into slavery, and they hadn't cared what became of him after that. They just wanted him out of their lives, for they hated him.

Now the tables were turned. There stood Joseph, no longer the little boy they had thrown into a pit. He was now second only to the Pharaoh and was so trusted that the king had put the nation's checkbook in his hand.

Joseph could have smiled at his brothers in that moment and said, as so many do, "Pay back time!" He could have had them all killed or imprisoned. He could have sold them into slavery. He could have tortured them slowly. But Joseph did none of these things. What he did do has amazed people ever since:

> *Joseph said to them, "Do not be afraid, for am I in the place of God? But as for you, you meant evil against me; but God meant it for good, in order to bring it about as it is this day, to save many people alive. Now therefore, do not be afraid; I will provide for you and your little ones." And he comforted them and spoke kindly to them.* Genesis 50:19-21

Joseph chose not to seek revenge, for He saw God at work in his circumstances. He chose to look beyond the actions of his brothers and others and to concentrate on the results that God had brought about in his life, and in the lives of many others as a result. God had used the jealousy of his brothers, for he would never have gotten where he was if he had gone his own way.

As a child, Joseph had been rather spoiled by his father. He might have looked at travel brochures of Cairo, but living in Egypt was not part of his plan. It was the farthest thing from Joseph's mind, but God knew that the lad must somehow get there.

There are places you will never go and people you will never meet unless God arranges circumstances in your life to direct you in a way other than you have planned. If you don't believe that His choice is good for you, then you'll start feeling like a victim, and when you start feeling like a victim, you'll begin to beat your donkey. But remember, as long as you're willing to remain a victim, you'll never be a victor.

You can insist on going the way that seems right to you, but is it right to God? Is it the way He would lead you? If your way is not God's way, then negative circumstances will begin to escalate in your life. You can look for it, for it will surely come.

God is redemptive, and His actions toward you will always be redemptive. He does not want to destroy you, but to redeem you. If your circumstances are negative, then know that God is trying to accomplish a redemptive work in your life. He is trying to set you back on a right path.

THE CASE OF THE THREE HEBREW CHILDREN

Sometimes God desires to deliver you, not *from* the fiery furnace, but *in* the fiery furnace. This was the case for Daniel's three companions.

King Nebuchadnezzar had set up a golden statue, and when Shadrach, Meshach and Abed-nego refused to worship it, they were brought before the king:

> *Nebuchadnezzar spoke, saying to them, "Is it true, Shadrach, Meshach, and Abed-Nego, that you do not serve my gods or worship the gold image which I have set up? Now if you are ready at the time you hear the sound of the horn, flute, harp, lyre, and psaltery, in symphony with all kinds of music, and you fall down and worship the image which I have made, good! But if you do not worship, you shall be cast immediately into the midst of a burning fiery furnace. And who is*

Circumstances

the god who will deliver you from my hands?"
Shadrach, Meshach, and Abed-Nego answered and
said to the king, "O Nebuchadnezzar, we have no need
to answer you in this matter. If that is the case, our
God whom we serve is able to deliver us from the burn-
ing fiery furnace, and He will deliver us from your
hand, O king. But if not, let it be known to you, O
king, that we do not serve your gods, nor will we wor-
ship the gold image which you have set up."

Daniel 3:14-18

"But if not." What powerful words! These three men
knew that God would deliver them; they just did not
know how or when. When they were cast into the furnace, they were unharmed. Instead, they met with One
who was *"like the Son of God"* (Daniel 3:25). As a result,
Shadrach, Meshach and Abed-nego were promoted by
the king, and a decree was issued to punish anyone who
might speak against their God.

We pray and we pray for God to deliver us from the
fierce flames, but sometimes this is not God's best for
us. We have a strange belief that if anything negative is
happening in our lives, God must be displeased with
us. But this is not always the case. Sometimes the things
that happen to us are for our own promotion, and sometimes they happen for the furtherance of the Kingdom
of God.

THE CASE OF STEPHEN AND PAUL

Stephen was a deacon in the local church in the first
century. He preached just one recorded sermon, and his

hearers stoned him to death. Some have surmised that he missed God or was out of God's will. "Obviously he wasn't called by God," some would say. "If he had been, they wouldn't have killed him after only one message." The Bible, however, tells a very different story.

First, it tells us that Stephen was a man of faith:

And they chose Stephen, a man full of faith and the Holy Spirit.
And Stephen, full of faith and power, did great wonders and signs among the people.   Acts 6:5 and 8

Stephen was a faith-filled, Spirit-filled man of God, and while it is true that the situation God placed him in cost him his life, we must consider the result. Stephen's death was the key to the conversion of the Apostle Paul, and the key to global evangelism.

We are much too quick to judge circumstances. There are many things that we may not understand, and we may form our opinions about them; but, quite frankly, the Father has not asked for our opinion. Leave it with God.

About half of Paul's life was spent in jail. If he were alive today, we would say, "Well, obviously he has missed God. After all, if Paul were in God's will, he would have his own television program. He would be featured at all the hottest Christian conferences. He would have a tape-of-the-month and a magazine of his own."

There is nothing wrong with any of these things, but it is wrong for us to judge success by them. When we see those who are struggling, facing trials and encountering financial difficulties, it is wrong for us to dismiss them as being out of God's will. God never said, "By their situations you will know them." It's what we do in our individual situations that counts.

The danger of being circumstance-directed, without the balance of the other six witnesses or principles, is that you can become sense-oriented. The Word of God commands us to *"walk by faith, not by sight."*

If you let circumstance say to you, "This is good," or "This is bad," then you will always be sight-ruled. You will frequently miss God's best for you if you are primarily guided by the situations of your life. You need the inner witness, the scriptural confirmation, the true prophetic witness and godly counsel to make you know that you are totally in the will of God.

Only one Person ever did everything right, and that was Jesus. They crucified Him, but the result is wonderful. He said:

And I, if I am lifted up from the earth, will draw all peoples to Myself.   John 12:32

Because of the circumstances to which Christ was willing to yield, He brought millions of people of all ages to Himself. And *"of His kingdom there will be no end"* (Luke 1:33).

Like Elijah, allow circumstances to confirm you in your path. Like Shadrach, Meshach and Abed-nego, allow God to use your circumstances to His glory. Like Gideon, prove God's direction by circumstance. But do not follow after it like Balaam did, against wisdom. Use circumstance, but also use wisdom. This is an important principle in *God's Guidance System*.

CHAPTER 8

THE PEACE OF GOD

For God is not the author of confusion but of peace, as in all the churches of the saints.

1 Corinthians 14:33

The sixth element of *God's Guidance System* is His peace. The peace of God is central to the workings of God, to His personality. In fact, the Scriptures call Him *"the God of Peace"*:

Now THE GOD OF PEACE be with you all. Amen.

Romans 15:33

And THE GOD OF PEACE will crush Satan under your feet shortly. The grace of our Lord Jesus Christ be with you. Amen.

Romans 16:20

The things which you learned and received and heard and saw in me, these do, and THE GOD OF PEACE will be with you.

Philippians 4:9

This *"God of peace"* (see also 1 Thessalonians 5:23 and Hebrews 13:20) dwells within you and me. We can know and walk in His peace, and we can learn to be guided, in part, by that peace.

There are two different kinds of peace mentioned in the Scriptures. If we fail to distinguish between the two, then we will find it difficult to be guided by God's peace. The first peace we find in the Bible is peace *with* God. The second peace is the peace *of* God.

PEACE *WITH* GOD

What does the Word of God say about our having peace *with* Him?

> *Therefore, having been justified by faith, we have PEACE WITH GOD through our Lord Jesus Christ.*
> Romans 5:1

Peace *with* God is a benefit and a privilege. It is given to every person who has asked Jesus Christ to be his Lord and Savior. Paul wrote:

> *And you, who once were alienated and enemies in your mind by wicked works, yet now He has reconciled in the body of His flesh through death, to present you holy, and blameless, and above reproach in His sight; if indeed you continue in the faith, grounded and steadfast, and are not moved away from the hope of the gospel which you heard, which was preached to every creature under heaven, of which I, Paul, became a minister.* Colossians 1:21-23

The Peace of God

We were once *"alienated."* We were outsiders, shut out from the things of God. We were also *"enemies"* of God. But even though we were on the outside, at war with God, He planned a way for us to be *"reconciled"* to Him. His great love reached out to us *"while we were still sinners"* (Romans 5:8). God brought us to Himself and gave us the gift of repentance. He pulled us from the kingdom of darkness to place us into the Kingdom of light.

We are no longer on the outside looking in. He has brought us inside to live with Him. Before we were born again, we were God's enemies. We didn't think like Him. We didn't act like Him. Everything we did was self-seeking. Like most people, we had almost a total disregard for God before salvation. Paul put it this way to the Gentile believers at Ephesus:

> *At that time you were without Christ, being aliens from the commonwealth of Israel and strangers from the covenants of promise, having no hope and without God in the world. But now in Christ Jesus you who once were far off have been brought near by the blood of Christ. For He Himself is our peace, who has made both one, and has broken down the middle wall of separation.* Ephesians 2:12-14

We were once without hope and *"without God."* Thank God that He provided a way out of such an existence! *"But now in Christ Jesus you who were far off from God have been made near by the blood of Christ."* Through the blood of Jesus Christ we are no longer *"enemies"* of God. We are no longer opposing God. And God is not angry with us. If you are a child of God, if Christ is your Lord and

149

Savior, if the Spirit of Christ dwells within you, then you are at peace with God.

No more is there enmity between you and God. You are no longer at war against Him; instead, you have *"peace with God."*

THE PEACE *OF* GOD

The second kind of peace, the peace *of* God, is for every believer. We see this in Paul's writings to the Colossians:

> *And let THE PEACE OF GOD rule in your hearts, to which also you were called in one body; and be thankful.* Colossians 3:15

We enter into peace *with* God at salvation. It is this peace *with* God that makes possible the peace *of* God within His children. You cannot know the peace *of* God unless you have experienced peace *with* God.

The peace *of* God can help to guide those who are at peace *with* God. This is a very powerful part of *God's Guidance System*. His peace in your heart can guide you in making decisions and in gaining direction for your life and the life of your family members — if you allow it to do so. Paul wrote:

> *The kingdom of God is not eating and drinking, but righteousness and peace and joy in the Holy Spirit.* Romans 14:17

The Kingdom of God is not the outward, physical reality. It's not how things look on the outside. It is *"righteousness and peace and joy in the Holy Spirit."* What is this righteousness? We know that this does not refer to any righteousness that might be of ourselves; rather, it is the righteousness of God. Righteousness is the peace *with* God that we receive through the blood of Jesus Christ. When you have this kind of peace, joy will also be added to you.

When you have lost your joy or your peace in life, you must retrace your steps. Where were you when you lost your peace? When did you stop knowing the peace of God? If you will look honestly at your life and evaluate it, you will probably be able to locate a point at which you said or did something that caused the peace *of* God to leave you. God didn't leave you, and your peace *with* God did not end. Only the peace *of* God left. You need to go back to that point, repent and make any reparations needed, so that you can be restored in God. You don't want to live a single day without His peace.

Joy is a natural outflow of the Kingdom of God. If you are not walking in joy, then somewhere you are missing the Kingdom in your life and in your walk with God. One of the best witnesses that we have in this world, to those who come into contact with us, is our joy and our peace. People will notice these two at work in our lives.

God wants His peace to *"rule in [our] hearts."* This is not the peace *with* God. That has already been given. The peace *of* God is to rule in my heart. The original Greek word here translated "rule" has the meaning of "umpire, referee, or govern." In other words, "Let the peace of God be the referee in your life."

God's Guidance System

THE UMPIRE

In a baseball game the umpire stands behind the catcher. The pitcher throws the ball to the batter, and the umpire judges the pitch — if the batter doesn't hit the ball. Is it a ball or a strike? If the pitch is good, the umpire calls it a strike. If it's not, he calls it a ball.

There are also base umpires. If a player is running to a base, and the ball is thrown to get him out, he might slide into the base. In the midst of the action, the umpire is there to watch and to judge. He decides whether the player is safe or out.

This is how the peace of God works in your life. God wants us to listen to the Holy Spirit, Him who brings peace into our hearts. We must let that peace (or that lack of peace, as is sometimes the case) become the umpire to call the balls and the strikes of our lives.

When you are beginning to go in a particular direction and the umpire inside you says, "Safe," you can walk in confidence, knowing that what you are doing is right and that your direction is in keeping with God's will. If it happens, it will be because the Holy Spirit is with you and because His peace in you is a witness to God's will.

If, however, you hear the Umpire of Life say, "Out," then you must not try to press through against His will. Anything that you obtain by pressing through His will and bypassing that peace, is not legally obtained. You might get it, but you will suffer in the process.

Don't get the wrong idea. God's guidance is not intended to put you in bondage. It is there to protect you and to keep you out of bondage.

The Peace of God

THE FULL MEANING OF PEACE

The Hebrew word for peace, as most of us know, is *shalom*, and this word is used as a typical Jewish or Israeli greeting. The meaning of *shalom*, however, goes much deeper than the meaning our English word "peace" usually carries. When we think of peace, we think of being free from strife or from bondage. *Shalom* means that, too, but it also means "prosperity, happiness, success, security and safety." This is the kind of peace that God desires to be working in your life. He wants you to be free from strife; He wants you to be secure; He wants you to prosper; and He wants you to be happy.

Some of us have been so beaten down by tradition and legalism that we find it difficult to believe that God might want to bless us. Sometimes we think or act as though He were out to trick us. *This certainly couldn't be from God*, we think. *It's too good. In fact, this is just what I wanted. And if I'm not suffering, not going through some adversity, it surely can't be God.*

We sometimes think that we can prove our love for God by going through difficult times. But sometimes serving God is just a matter of common sense, which this type of thinking is not. Instead of allowing thoughts that lead to strife, we need to run after peace. We should *"pursue the things which make for peace"*:

> *Therefore let us pursue the things which make for peace and the things by which one may edify another.*
> Romans 14:19

"Pursue ... peace!" Run after it. Be serious about catching it.

Is your home, your marriage, a place of peace? Do you follow a course in your conversation that leads to peace in your marriage and in your family instead of strife and conflict? This is God's command to each of us.

I believe one reason some husbands or wives are not anxious to go home is because they know they will walk right into an oppressive atmosphere. We must transform the atmosphere of our homes through praise or through the kindness of speech. Our words and actions should build up and edify one another, and peace should reign in our homes.

Many people hold onto their frustrations all day long. Then, when they finally get to be with the one they love and care for the most in life, it all comes out. Instead of meeting their loved one with open arms and with words of gratitude, everything explodes out of them in an ugly, angry rush.

Venting

These days we call this phenomenon "venting." If you have a working fireplace, then you know what a flue or vent is. It is used to control the amount of air that draws the smoke up the chimney. Your vent can keep the fire hot, or it can be used to put the fire out. If you do not adjust your vent just right, then the smoke will not go up the chimney and out into the atmosphere; it will fill your house. Your eyes will burn and your throat will become very sore. It isn't a very pleasant experience.

The Peace of God

As children of God, we need to control our vents. I don't mean that we should never bring up anything negative or never let anyone know about the bad things that happen to us. That's not healthy. But we must have good, honest, levelheaded sharing. We can share the things we feel, but we cannot pour them out upon others. We have no right at all to take our own anger and frustration and impatience and pour them out on anyone, least of all the ones to whom we are closest. We should be sharing the life of Christ with them, not the frustrations that we have stored up all day.

When we do share things with one another, we must do it with the attitude that possibly we are the ones who are wrong. This will prevent much of the strife that commonly comes into a relationship when we are too proud to admit that we might be wrong and that someone else might be right.

Once my wife Viv and I returned home from a trip late on a Saturday night. On Sunday we went to church and had a great service. We rested that day, relaxing together. On Monday, I knew, I would have to think about dealing with some problems we were facing in our family.

I went to the church that day and tried to keep myself busy, but these problems were uppermost in my mind.

Meanwhile, Viv had gone out to a sale. Her intention was to buy some things to brighten up our bedroom — some new sheets, a comforter, some curtains. When I came home, she wanted to surprise me, hoping to make me feel better about things.

All day the thought of our problems kept building in

my mind until, at the end of the day, when I got home, I was not a very pleasant companion. When I made my way into the bedroom that night to get ready for bed, my mind was so engrossed in my problems that I didn't even notice what she had done to the room.

She was waiting for me to say, "Hey, honey, the room looks nice," but I wasn't saying anything. I was too wrapped up in myself.

Finally, she gave up hope that I would notice and asked, "Do you like the comforter?"

Then I saw it for the first time and said, "Oh, that's nice."

When I started to get into bed, I rolled the comforter back and there were the new sheets and pillowcases. Looking back on what happened next, it didn't take much ingenuity to know that I should have said, "Honey, I appreciate your thinking about me and doing this to make me feel better because you understand what I'm going through." Instead, what came out of my mouth was, "How much did all this cost?"

I knew immediately that I had wounded her, and I had. We both rolled over and went to sleep. The next morning I took her in my arms and said, "Honey, I'm sorry. Please forgive me. I shouldn't have responded that way. It shouldn't have mattered. It was not an issue of cost at all. The most important thing was that you were thinking of me. I was so absorbed in my own thoughts that I could hardly notice what you had done." And that's the cause of most of our problem: each of us is thinking only of himself.

The Bible gives us totally different instructions. We are not to follow after our own desires; we are to *follow after the things that make for peace."* Peace is the absence of strife, but how can we follow after the absence of something? We cannot. We are to follow after *"the things that make for peace,"* the things that bring peace, meaning security, happiness, prosperity, and joy.

From time to time there will be confrontations in our lives, but these do not have to turn into battles. Don't stir up strife in the midst of the confrontation. Don't say that one thing that you know is guaranteed to inflame and to make things worse. Be the one who pours forth peace. Be a peacemaker in every situation.

Another Scripture echoes this thought:

> *Pursue peace with all people, and holiness, without which no one will see the Lord.*   Hebrews 12:14

"Pursue peace with all people." Think about that. We are to do whatever causes peace with everyone — not just good people, not just the people we like, but *"with all people."*

DISTURBING THE PEACE

There are people who are known as disturbers of the peace, and under our legal system, they can be arrested. Disturbing the peace is a crime. We should periodically examine ourselves to see if we have become criminals in this sense. Don't be guilty of disturbing the peace, and don't allow others to disturb your peace.

Is someone disturbing your peace? They might be coming into your home in person, by phone, by television, radio, or the Internet, or by some other means. They may come bearing gossip and sowing discord. They may be slandering, bringing negativity or an evil report. Arrest that person. Remove the welcome mat for them from your front door, from your mind and from your heart.

If you must, change your telephone number. This may sound harsh, but you need to give some people notice and cut them loose from your life. Whatever it takes to follow peace, that's what you need to do.

James has another strong word on this subject:

> *For where envy and self-seeking exist, confusion and every evil thing are there.* James 3:16

Gossip and slander are just the tip of the iceberg. Combined with them are *"confusion and every evil thing."* Surely we don't need any more confusion than we already have around us. We must, therefore, stop these things dead in their tracks. Don't gossip, and don't allow yourself to listen to any gossip. Don't envy others. And (this is the hard one) be dead to self rather than self-seeking. Our flesh hates to hear that, but it is the only way we will ever really know the peace of God.

James did not stop there. He showed us where confusion dwells. Then he went on to speak of being peaceable in wisdom and action:

> *But the wisdom that is from above is first pure, then peaceable, gentle, willing to yield, full of mercy and good fruits, without partiality and without hypocrisy. Now the fruit of righteousness is sown in peace by those who make peace.* James 3:17-18

The Peace of God

If you are unsure of how to obtain this kind of wisdom, you may recall God's earlier promise in the same book of the Bible:

> *If any of you lacks wisdom, let him ask of God, who gives to all liberally and without reproach, and it will be given to him.*   James 1:5

God wants you to be wise in *"the things that make for peace."* It is in the atmosphere of peace that God can speak to us. Many Christians don't yet realize this. They seem to think that if they pray longer, louder and faster, then God will answer quicker.

QUIETNESS BEFORE GOD

People often say, "I thought I heard God say ..." But we need to know for certain if what we are hearing is from Him or not. Quite often, if we expect to hear exactly what He has said, we must spend some time in quietness before Him. When Elijah wanted to hear God, he didn't hear Him in the earthquake. He didn't hear Him in the fire. He didn't hear Him in the whirlwind. He heard Him in a still, small voice, a voice that spoke into his heart. The psalmist wrote:

> *Be still, and know that I am God;*
> *I will be exalted among the nations,*
> *I will be exalted in the earth!*   Psalm 46:10

The New American Standard Bible translates this verse: *"Cease striving and know that I am God."* Since the

159

word striving is understood, the literal translation would be: *"Cease, and know that I am God."* Cease what? It really doesn't say, and it doesn't matter. Just cease. Cease whatever is bringing the disturbance. Cease everything for a time if need be, stop doing and just be. Then, in the quietness, know that He is God. Quit striving. Get out from under all pressure, and then you can see and hear God. You'll never hear Him in the midst of confusion.

Some cry out, "I simply must have an answer right now! My life depends on it!" Maybe it does in your own eyes, but you can rest in knowing that the One who created you has a good idea of what your life is dependent upon.

Perhaps God has placed you in this situation for a purpose. Sometimes we hear so much teaching about God's goodness and His love, His provision and His caring, that we forget that He has a purpose for us beyond our comfort. Maybe He has something for you to learn in that difficult place, something you have not yet grown still enough to grasp. Let quietness reveal God to you.

GOD'S PEACE GUIDES US

The peace of God will do three things for us. It will guide, it will govern, and it will guard.

We are to follow peace because it will guide us — in any decision, in any relationship, in any business deal, in any career change. If you are not sensing God's peace, then get off of the path you are on and trust God to help you find the right path. Those who are in the will of God experience perfect peace.

We cannot know everything; but we can know the One

who does, and when we are trying to make a decision, trying to follow God's direction, He gives us a guide, a sign, concerning which way we should go. He either gives or removes His peace from our hearts.

We have all heard people talk about the lack of God's peace. You've probably said these things yourself: "I just don't know. I don't really feel good about this. I just don't have any peace about this whole thing." When this happens, it is a good sign that God is talking to you and telling you not to proceed. He is guiding you through His peace.

GOD'S PEACE GOVERNS US

The peace of God is given to govern. When Paul said, *"Let the peace of God rule in your hearts,"* that word rule means "to govern." In terms of guidance, we first look to see if a situation violates the clear teaching of the Scriptures. If it does, we don't want to have anything to do with it anyway. It's automatically out. But what happens if there is no clear teaching of scripture concerning a particular situation? Then we have another way to help us get our confirmation: peace or the lack of peace.

How do you feel about this matter? When you have prayed about this situation, did you have a sense of peace about it or are you still unsure? If you have prayed, but you are still unsure, then wait. Give the Lord time, waiting in quietness to know what He says. If you still do not have a peace about it, then, by all means, don't proceed.

Sometimes we honestly cannot say how we feel about a situation. Sometimes we are too emotionally bound up in the matter to tell whether we have peace about it or not. One good source of help for you, if you are married, is your spouse. If he or she is tuned to the Spirit, this can be a help in discerning the will of God. Wives seem to be especially good at this, as women are usually more intuitive in their thinking than men. We need to listen to one another in this regard.

Suppose a wife says to her husband, "I don't feel good about that person. He keeps hounding you with his business opportunities, but I don't feel right about it," or "I don't feel good about that new co-worker of yours. Do you have to spend so much time with her on the job?"

It might be the other way around and the husband might say something like this to his wife. In either case, nothing blatantly wrong seems to be evident, but if a partner has no peace about a situation, it should be, for us, reason to reconsider.

We have a tendency to say to each other, "I'm not infallible." While that is true, we must be willing to give each other the benefit of the doubt and, by doing so, we will sometimes save ourselves a lot of heartache.

The wonderful thing about peace as a form of guidance is that you don't have to go looking for it. It's either there or it isn't. If you keep your relationship strong with the Lord and stay in the Spirit, you will know what is right and what is not.

When we let the peace of God govern our lives and actions, we are careful not to do anything that jeopardizes that peace. We try not to allow our words or our actions to take us out of that realm of peace. And we continually ask the Lord to make His way clear to us, submitting ourselves to the righteous rule of peace.

The Peace of God

The Bible likens the relationship between God and man to that between man and wife. Both are covenantal relationships, and in both, we can never be successful unless we come into agreement with the other party.

For instance, it would not be a good idea for most people to go out and buy a new car without first consulting their spouse. It is not right to do something first and later try to get our spouses to adjust to our unilateral decision and have peace about it. It doesn't work that way.

"Well, bless God," some might say, "I'm walking in faith." If what you are doing is causing unrest in your spouse or children or if it's troubling your own soul, then you are not walking in faith. You're walking in selfishness.

The devil will always try to come to us and shake the peace we are feeling. If it really is the peace of God, however, the devil can shake all he wants and he won't be able to shake us loose from what God has put in our spirits.

Be careful not to violate the peace in your heart to build your ego or to appease your flesh. If you have made a wrong turn in this area, if you have gotten yourself into a bad situation, then back out as quickly as possible. If whatever you are involved in does not govern your heart with peace, then get out as fast as you can. In such cases, you cannot say, "I'll stick it out until I see if this goes bad." It will go bad, and you can count on that. God's peace is a sure sign of His will.

GOD'S PEACE GUARDS US

Finally, God's peace is to guard us. We can rejoice in

this fact, for it is the promise of God. To the Philippians, Paul wrote:

> *Be anxious for nothing, but in everything by prayer and supplication, with thanksgiving, let your requests be made known to God; and the peace of God, which surpasses all understanding, will guard [surround or protect] your hearts and minds through Christ Jesus.*
>
> Philippians 4:6-7

After you have prayed, after you have given God thanks, the peace of God will guard your mind, your heart and your decision. There is, however, an implicit warning: be careful not to ignore what God is showing you.

When Saul was king over Israel, he brought together three thousand men to fight the Philistines. The prophet Samuel, Saul's spiritual guide and mentor, had told him to wait seven days before attacking the Philistines. Samuel would meet Saul at that time and would offer up a sacrifice to the Lord before the men went to battle.

Seven days went by, and the Philistines were looking more fierce each day. Saul observed them organizing and amassing their armies, and so did his men. The result was that the soldiers of Israel, one by one, began to flee.

What should Saul do in a case like this? He was losing his army before the battle had even begun, and Samuel had not yet returned. In the end, Saul did what many of us might have done in this situation. He took matters into his own hands, going ahead with the sacrifice without the presence of the prophet and priest.

The Old Testament Scriptures clearly stated that only

a priest could offer a sacrifice before the Lord. The Mosaic Law and other levitical statutes were very clear on the subject, and there was no room for any misinterpretation. Saul, however, was desperate. In this moment, he was not considering the Scriptures. He could think only of the need to rush quickly into battle. Instead of examining the Scriptures to see whether his planned course of action would be pleasing to God, he allowed the pressure of the situation to remove the guard of peace from his heart and his mind. And he consequently missed God.

Ignoring sacred Law, Saul went ahead and offered up the burnt offering on his own. It is significant to note that God interrupted him before he could offer up the peace offering, as he had intended:

> *Now it happened, as soon as he had finished presenting the burnt offering, that Samuel came; and Saul went out to meet him, that he might greet him. And Samuel said, "What have you done?"*
> *And Saul said, "When I saw that the people were scattered from me, and that you did not come within the days appointed, and that the Philistines gathered together at Michmash, then I said, 'The Philistines will now come down on me at Gilgal, and I have not made supplication to the LORD.' Therefore I felt compelled, and offered a burnt offering."*   1 Samuel 13:10-12

The language of the King James Version in verse 12 is revealing: Saul said, "*I forced myself ... and offered a burnt offering.*" We cannot afford to be forced in anything. God does not operate in this way. If we respond to outside forces, rather than to the clear leading of the Lord, we will find ourselves, like Saul, cast out from any position.

What a poor excuse Saul used! "The pressure got to me, and I couldn't wait any longer. Somebody had to do something, so I took action." It is sad to say that many of us are moved in the same way. The Word of God shows us:

> *But those who wait on the LORD*
> *Shall renew their strength;*
> *They shall mount up with wings like eagles,*
> *They shall run and not be weary,*
> *They shall walk and not faint.*   Isaiah 40:31

Saul should have known better. He allowed the existing circumstances to speak to him. He did not speak to the circumstances. When he allowed himself to be carried away by what he thought the circumstances demanded, he violated the peace of God in his heart.

What might Saul have done instead? I believe that he should have spoken to the circumstances. He should have said, "I don't know God's plan, but I do know that I'm under authority. I am under Samuel's orders. I don't know why Samuel hasn't returned yet, but I do know one thing. God did not bring me here to destroy me."

God was testing Saul's heart to see if he would stand or not, and when he was moved by fear and decided to take things into his own hands, God knew that he was not the man for the job. This should teach us all that if God is not moving in a situation, we can't accomplish anything by trying to force things.

When Samuel arrived, he rebuked the king:

The Peace of God

And Samuel said to Saul, "You have done foolishly. You have not kept the commandment of the LORD your God, which He commanded you. For now the LORD would have established your kingdom over Israel forever. But now your kingdom shall not continue. The LORD has sought for Himself a man after His own heart, and the LORD has commanded him to be commander over His people, because you have not kept what the LORD commanded you."

1 Samuel 13:13-14

Samuel didn't waste any words, but let King Saul know, "Your foolishness has cost you the kingdom."

Many of us, when faced with serious choices have also violated the peace of God in our hearts, and when it has happened, we, like Saul, have suffered great loss because of it.

David knew what it was to lose one's joy. That is why he was so emphatic when he prayed:

Restore to me the joy of Your salvation.

Psalm 51:12

When we make wrong choices and violate the peace of God in our hearts, we feel condemned and intimidated, and we imagine that God will no longer hear our prayers or speak to us. Many, in this situation, stop going to church and break off many of their close Christian relationships. They are confused and in turmoil and don't know which way to turn. Some never recover from their loss.

God's Guidance System

DON'T BLAME SATAN

Most of us blame the devil for all our woes, when it hasn't been the devil's fault at all. If we insist on running God's red lights, and we force our way through life, doing things that we sense are not God's perfect will for our lives, we are opening the door to the devil and giving him the right to steal our peace. He only comes by invitation.

What can we do in such cases? First, we must repent, for what we have done has grieved the heart of God. Secondly, we must stop what we are doing that is wrong and turn back to God's plan for our lives. When we take this action, our peace can be quickly restored. God knows how to redeem every situation.

Once, when I was sitting in the front seat of an airliner, we experienced some severe cross winds during the flight. As we were getting ready to land, the door to the cockpit was opened, and I could watch what the pilots were doing. About that time we hit another crosswind and the plane dipped. I heard a computerized voice from the cockpit saying, "Pull up, pull up." I prayed, "Yes, God. Pull up, please." The Lord heard my cry, and we landed safely.

If that pilot had ignored the warning that he was coming to ground too fast, it might have been disastrous for all of us. Thank God he heeded the warning and addressed the emergency.

If you have warnings going off in your life, if the peace of God has gone from your heart, that is a danger signal that you cannot afford to ignore. Do whatever you must to address the situation — before it is eternally too late.

The Peace of God

If you will heed the peace of God that is guarding your heart, God will honor your faith. He will honor your obedience, and life will go well for you.

We can have peace with God through the blood of Jesus shed on the cross of Calvary, and if we have, for any reason, lost that peace, we can recover it. John's words on confession of sin were not written to the ungodly, but to the Church:

> *If we confess our sins, He is faithful and just to forgive us our sins and to cleanse us from all unrighteousness.*   1 John 1:9

When we have God's righteousness, we will have peace, and the peace of God will bring forth joy in our lives. This is an important principle of *God's Guidance System* that we simply must not ignore.

CHAPTER 9

THE PROVISION OF GOD

The steps of a good man are ordered by the LORD,
And He delights in his way.
Though he fall, he shall not be utterly cast down;
For the LORD upholds him with His hand.

Psalm 37:23-24

God delights in ordering our way, and in seeing us take the steps He has ordained. That is why He has given us this guidance system, to keep us from making fatal mistakes. The final principle of *God's Guidance System* is His provision.

I read that in a survey that included Christians and non-Christians, the favorite scripture of both was the same. It was David's beloved 23rd Psalm:

The LORD is my shepherd; I shall not want.

Psalm 23:1

This Psalm has blessed so many people because it shows the goodness of our God. It shows Him as a God of provision, One who gives good things to men. When He is our Shepherd, we have everything we need, and we have nothing to fear.

Hudson Taylor was a missionary in China during the 1850s and was the founder of the China Inland Mission. The influence of this mission did not cease with the death of its founder, but has effected revival in China even until the present. One of Taylor's foundational principles was that if God was guiding, then He would provide all that was needed. I believe this is the final confirmation as to whether we are on the right track in God's guidance. Is God providing? If so, it is a practical demonstration of His guidance. And if He is not providing, then we have reason to pause and examine our paths.

GOD PROVIDED FOR NOAH TO BUILD THE ARK

God's Word is filled with remarkable demonstrations of this principle. For instance, when God commanded Noah to build the ark, He provided what Noah needed to accomplish the task. God gave Noah the wisdom to be able to build the ark, and He gave him very specific directions concerning its building. He provided Noah the resources to build such a large ark — the wood, the tools, the other supplies, and He also provided the time, freeing Noah and his sons for one hundred and twenty years to finish the job.

Many people, even Christians, have a great fear of death and dying, but I have good news. Whatever God has called us to do, whatever our purpose, whatever our destiny on this Earth, God will provide the time we need to fulfill it. If we are walking in the purpose and the will

The Provision of God

of God, as He has directed and called us, then death is not something we should fear. If God has called us to a certain purpose, then He will provide the material, mental and spiritual resources to complete that purpose, and the time we need as well. Paul wrote to Timothy:

The time of my departure is at hand. I have fought the good fight, I have finished the race, I have kept the faith. 2 Timothy 4:6-7

Those who opposed Paul had been trying to kill him for many years, but they could not get rid of him until he had finished his course. When he had fulfilled his destiny, then God said, "All right, child. You can come on home now."

God is a builder. If He lives inside you, then you have a drive to accomplish something in life. If He dwells within you, then you have a thirst for a meaningful work here on Earth. You long to accomplish your purpose, to fulfill your destiny.

God is intent on building His Kingdom, and He permits His children to share in the work. He is building His Kingdom within each of us, and He wants us to help build it in men's hearts everywhere.

FEAR OF WHAT MIGHT BE

Far too often, when we think of our dreams of the future, we are afraid of what might be. I grew up in the South, and my mother used to say, "Might? Mites grow on chickens." She was talking about the tiny microscopic animal life that lives on birds. Our "mights" are just like that. They're microscopic as far as life itself is concerned. In order to focus on them, you must take your eyes off of God. It is He who we should be magnifying and not the "mights."

If you have ever looked at a flea under a microscope, you know that it looks like some terrible prehistoric monster. If you look at a flea, however, with the naked eye, it seems like nothing. If you are outdoors and a flea lands on your arm, you might not even notice it. You certainly wouldn't call an intercessors group or ask the elders of the church to come and pray for you. A flea is so insignificant that you just flick it off and go about your duties.

The majority of the things that we allow to hinder us from doing God's will are just as insignificant as fleas. When we take our eyes off God to focus on these inconsequential things, they seem to become bigger than God is. And that is what causes our fears.

The only thing that can hinder God's provision for your life is your own disobedience and rebellion. Outside of that, God will do whatever has to be done to see that you have all that you need. If God has to stop the sun and back it up ten degrees, He will do it. If He has to anoint and open the womb of a ninety-year-old woman, He will do it. If He has to multiply oil or loaves and fish to accomplish His purpose, He will do it.

To get in line for God's provision, first ask Him what you are to do, what you are to accomplish in life. As He gives you a sense of destiny, nurture it and ask God to increase it. A sense of destiny, of purpose, eliminates fear. If you know that you have a purpose in life, that there is something out there that God has called you to do, even though you have not yet fulfilled it, you will find no reason to be fearful.

We cannot be foolish, and we cannot be presumptuous, but we should not live in fear, either. If God has given us a promise in our lives, that promise will come to pass.

THREE NEAR-DEATH EXPERIENCES

I'm a prime example of this fact. Three times, in December 1995 and the first part of January of 1996, I was brought to death's door. I could easily have slipped through. I knew, however, that my destiny and my purpose had not yet been fulfilled, so I was not afraid.

I had to undergo heart surgery to repair a faulty valve. My doctor said to me, "God wants that heart to tick even more than you do, so if it is God's will, as we believe, when we start it pumping again, it will start." And it did.

A few days after that, however, an artery in my leg burst. I could have died then, too, but it was not God's time, and I survived.

Then the medical team working on me accidentally used tainted blood. This sent me into convulsions and, again, nearly took my life. But I lived.

God had three opportunities in quick succession to say, "Welcome home, son"; the devil had three opportunities to say, "We're rid of that one"; but my destiny and purpose were not yet fulfilled, so I lived. We must never walk in fear, for we are called to walk in faith.

When God led the children of Israel into the wilderness, He provided for them. He sent them manna from

Heaven. He caused water to come forth from a rock. If God has brought you into a difficult place, then He will provide for you in that place, even if you are there for disciplinary reasons. You are still God's child, and He will provide for you.

God will give you grace and strength. He will make a way for you when there seems to be no way. He will prepare a table for you in the presence of your enemies. When it seems as though you cannot go any further and you are about to fall, He will provide His angels to take charge of you and to bear you up.

Fear not! God is your Savior. That is His nature. If there is anything in your life that can be saved, redeemed or restored, God will do it. He will pour out His life and His provision in abundance. That's the kind of God we serve.

The book of Genesis contains a beautiful foreshadowing of God's love for man and of His redemptive nature and purpose. It is the story of Abraham and Isaac.

ABRAHAM'S OFFERING OF ISAAC

Isaac was Abraham's son of promise. Abraham had waited a long time for Isaac, and he loved him greatly, yet God saw fit to test Abraham by asking for his only son:

> *Now it came to pass after these things that God tested Abraham, and said to him, "Abraham!"*
> *And he said, "Here I am."*
> *Then He said, "Take now your son, your only son Isaac, whom you love, and go to the land of Moriah,*

and offer him there as a burnt offering on one of the
mountains of which I shall tell you."
So Abraham rose early in the morning and saddled
his donkey, and took two of his young men with him,
and Isaac his son; and he split the wood for the burnt
offering, and arose and went to the place of which God
had told him.   Genesis 22:1-3

Abraham did not delay when he knew God's guidance for his life. Even though it was an extremely difficult task that God had set before for him, Abraham set out at once. He took with him everything he would need for his journey and for his sacrifice.

When God gives you something to do, have the heart of an Abraham. Go forth well prepared, and do not procrastinate about it. There is a saying common among some parents: delayed obedience is disobedience. We would do well to heed this in our walk with God.

As Abraham took that journey with his son, his heart must have been breaking at the enormity of what was being required of him. Nevertheless, he did not flinch in his obedience.

Finally, after a journey of three days that must have been grueling for the man of faith, they drew near to the mountain where the sacrifice would take place:

Then on the third day Abraham lifted his eyes and
saw the place afar off. And Abraham said to his young
men, "Stay here with the donkey; the lad and I will
go yonder and worship, and we will come back to you."
                                                Genesis 22:4-5

What faith! Abraham did not say, "I will come back to you," but *"[we] will come back."* He was trusting God with that which he valued most in life, and he was sure that God would not fail him.

After many years of waiting for God's promise to be fulfilled in the birth of Isaac, how would a nation now be raised up from Abraham through Isaac if Isaac was dead? Abraham could not have understood all this, but he knew that God was asking him to give Isaac back, and he knew that he must obey. He would follow God's leading — whatever it cost him personally:

> *So Abraham took the wood of the burnt offering and laid it on Isaac his son; and he took the fire in his hand, and a knife, and the two of them went together.*
> *But Isaac spoke to Abraham his father and said, "My father!"*
> *And he said, "Here I am, my son."*
> *Then he said, "Look, the fire and the wood, but where is the lamb for a burnt offering?"*
> *And Abraham said, "My son, God will provide for Himself the lamb for a burnt offering."*
> *So the two of them went together.*   Genesis 22:6-8

"God will provide for Himself." If He has asked for a sacrifice, then He will provide what is needed. We have nothing to fear in this regard.

A verse that is often quoted, but sometimes misunderstood is this:

> *I can do all things through Christ who strengthens me.*   Philippians 4:13

The Provision of God

Obviously, taken at face value, what this verse says cannot be true. I cannot fly on my own strength, I cannot eradicate poverty or homelessness, I cannot cure AIDS. I cannot do *"all things."* So what was Paul saying? A more literal translation of this verse might be:

I can do all that God asks of me through the power of Christ who is resident within me.

God will provide. If He has asked something of me, He will enable me to give it. I might not be able to do everything that I think up, but I can carry out every assignment given to me by God because He will provide what I need to do it.

I believe this is what Abraham was seeing. If God had called him to that sacrifice, then God would enable him to complete it. And He did just that:

Then they came to the place of which God had told him. And Abraham built an altar there and placed the wood in order; and he bound Isaac his son and laid him on the altar, upon the wood. And Abraham stretched out his hand and took the knife to slay his son.

But the Angel of the Lord called to him from heaven and said, "Abraham, Abraham!"

So he said, "Here I am."

And He said, "Do not lay your hand on the lad, or do anything to him; for now I know that you fear God, since you have not withheld your son, your only son, from Me."

Then Abraham lifted his eyes and looked, and there

behind him was a ram caught in a thicket by its horns. So Abraham went and took the ram, and offered it up for a burnt offering instead of his son. And Abraham called the name of the place, The-LORD-Will-Provide; as it is said to this day, "In the Mount of The LORD it shall be provided." Genesis 22:9-14

Abraham called that place Jehovah-Jireh, which means "the Lord will provide." What is it that you need right now? Finances? Food or clothing? Patience? Know that God sees what you need; He sees your circumstances; He sees your valley; and He never looks on a situation as a detached observer. He is a Provider; He is aware of your need; and He has made provision in every area — spiritually, physically, financially, emotionally, socially and politically.

WHEN GOD DOES NOT PROVIDE

God is our Provider, but there is another side to the story. Just as the manifestation or the possession of God's provision is a form of His guidance, so the restraint of His provision is also a form of His guidance. God will provide, but in order to guide you in the proper way, there are times when He will restrain you by withholding His provision.

We hear people say, "If I had a million dollars, I would do this and I would do that. I'd go here, and I'd go there. I'd build this, and I'd buy that." But maybe that isn't what God wants them to do, and just maybe that is why He is withholding the money. Sometimes withholding money from us (or whatever else we might need) is how the Lord stops us from going on ahead of what He has spoken to us to do.

God is not unfair, and we should never covet the blessings He gives to others. If He is blessing someone else more than He is blessing us, He has a purpose for them that is different than His purpose for us. It is even possible that He knows that another person will be more faithful with what He has given than we will.

God is faithful to restrain us to keep us from something that isn't His will. No matter how much we have wanted a position in the church, no matter how much we have thought that we should be on a certain ministry team or worship team, God has the right to restrain us in some way if what we are doing is not His perfect will or if it is not yet His time.

Jesus taught us that a true father always provides for his child:

> *Or what man is there among you who, if his son asks for bread, will give him a stone? Or if he asks for a fish, will he give him a serpent? If you then, being evil, know how to give good gifts to your children, how much more will your Father who is in heaven give good things to those who ask Him!*
>
> Matthew 7:9-11

Paul gave the same teaching:

> *But if anyone does not provide for his own, and especially for those of his household, he has denied the faith and is worse than an unbeliever.* 1 Timothy 5:8

God is more than a good father. He is the perfect Father, and if a good father takes care of His children, how much more our Heavenly Father. One man of God discovered this when he came face to face with an evil king.

ELIJAH VS. THE WICKED KING AHAB

Ahab was one of the more wicked in a series of wicked kings who ruled Israel. Elijah, a prophet of God, was called upon to face him. God had warned His people:

> *Take heed to yourselves, lest your heart be deceived, and you turn aside and serve other gods and worship them, lest the LORD's anger be aroused against you, and He shut up the heavens so that there be no rain, and the land yield no produce, and you perish quickly from the good land which the LORD is giving you.*
>
> Deuteronomy 11:16-17

The Law had set forth several times not only the promises of God but also the consequences for disobedience to Him. These laws were well known to the people of Israel. When Ahab set up a temple and an altar to Baal, the inevitable happened. The heavens were shut up and there was no rain. Elijah was called upon to proclaim this judgment to the king:

> *And Elijah the Tishbite, of the inhabitants of Gilead, said to Ahab, "As the LORD God of Israel lives, before whom I stand, there shall not be dew nor rain these years, except at my word."*
> *Then the word of the LORD came to him, saying, "Get*

*away from here and turn eastward, and hide by the
Brook Cherith, which flows into the Jordan. And it
will be that you shall drink from the brook, and I have
commanded the ravens to feed you there." So he went
and did according to the word of the LORD, for he went
and stayed by the Brook Cherith, which flows into the
Jordan.*   1 Kings 17:1-5

Elijah was to be fed by ravens, although, according to
the Mosaic Law, ravens were unclean birds. The fact that
ravens had touched meat was reason enough for any Jew
to refuse to eat it. Besides, how could anyone know
where that meat had come from? This was not a very
appetizing prospect for Elijah, but God used ravens to
sustain his life, and the prophet did not reject the provision because of the way in which it was to be given. We
must be careful not to miss our blessing by rejecting the
package it comes in.

Elijah was provided for ... for a while, at least:

*The ravens brought him bread and meat in the morn-
ing, and bread and meat in the evening; and he drank
from the brook. And it happened after a while that the
brook dried up, because there had been no rain in the
land.*   1 Kings 17:6-7

Is your brook drying up? Are you feeling that the provision of God for your life is passing away? If so, maybe
the Lord is ready to give you new instructions. Don't
become angry with God. Don't start kicking at the dirt
and saying, "Oh, this sorry, low-down brook! It's no good

for anything!" God has a purpose in all that He does. When one source fails, expect Him to provide another.

Life always brings change, and we must be able to change with it and be led by the Spirit of God in the midst of that change. We can't be getting angry at the brook, and we can't be getting angry at God. If we become still, we will be able to hear Him giving us new instructions. This is what happened to Elijah:

> *Then the word of the LORD came to him, saying,*
> *"Arise, go to Zarephath, which belongs to Sidon, and*
> *dwell there. See, I have commanded a widow there to*
> *provide for you."*   1 Kings 17:8-9

Before Elijah even left the brook, his provision in the next place was already prepared. If we just sit grumbling beside our brook, we may miss something wonderful. Let us be obedient to go forth into the provision that God has already made for us. Elijah did:

> *So he arose and went to Zarephath. And when he came*
> *to the gate of the city, indeed a widow was there gath-*
> *ering sticks. And he called to her and said, "Please*
> *bring me a little water in a cup, that I may drink."*
>   1 Kings 17:10

If God has really called us to start a church or a business, if He has really called us to do something or to go somewhere, then He will prepare the hearts of other people who are involved, and He will often do this even before we get there. We have no reason to strive or to manipulate people. We don't need nearly as much promotion or self-defense as we think. If this thing is of God, then He will prepare the hearts of the people, and this will be a confirmation of His call.

This is not a matter of how much revelation knowledge you have, of how strong the anointing is upon your life, or of how much natural ability you might possess. The question is simply: Did God call you? If He did, then *"[His] yoke is easy and [His] burden is light"* (Matthew 11:30). If He calls, He will also enable us to fulfill that call.

Elijah had been content at the brook, for the ravens were bringing his food and the water of the brook was supplying his drink. He was comfortable in God's provision. This was all the more remarkable when we remember that there was a drought in the land. No one in his right mind would want to leave the comfort of such a situation. Yet God called Elijah to do just that. The Father had something else for His prophet to do.

Elijah was reluctant to go. Things were going well for him there, and he had no way of knowing what awaited him in the next place. In the end, the only way the Lord could get His servant to leave was to dry up the brook, to take away Elijah's provision. So that is what He did.

In this way, God uses both provision and lack of provision to guide us. Sometimes He leads us into new green pastures by drying out the ones we're in now. This is where we need discernment, for sometimes Satan tries to come in and rob us of the provision of God. When this is the case, we must fight for what is ours. Sometimes the lack is of God, and is a sign that He is guiding us in a different direction. This is another of those occasions when it helps to have several types of confirmation to God's will, not just one. When your brook dries up, ask God for wisdom to discern what exactly is going on.

HUMAN PERSPIRATION VS. DIVINE PROVISION

Under Old Testament Law, the Levitical priests could not wear woolen undergarments. They had to wear linen. Why do you suppose that was? I believe it was because linen was cooler. Woolen underclothes would have caused them to perspire as they performed their duties, and perspiration symbolizes man's effort, man's striving to accomplish some work. God doesn't need your fleshly effort to help in any destiny that He has given you. Let us always remember His message to Zerubbabel:

> *So he answered and said to me:*
> *"This is the word of the LORD to Zerubbabel:*
> *'Not by might nor by power, but by My Spirit,'*
> *Says the LORD of hosts.' "*   Zechariah 4:6

God doesn't require our help in the area of provision. He is perfectly capable of supporting His family. If He has called you and you are wondering what lies ahead, remember this truth: Where God guides, He provides.

Often, God requires that we take a step of faith before we see the resources provided for our situation. But God does indeed provide everything we need, if we let Him do it.

Sometimes we pressure ourselves and those around us to have things that were not intended for us. I have seen local churches striving for finances for a ministry or for a building fund. They had all sorts of fund-raisers, tried to manipulate their members into giving more, suddenly began preaching a series of messages on tithing, giving and sacrifice. While there may be nothing wrong with any of these things, in and of themselves, when God is truly leading us, the financial provision should not be drenched with the sweat of human effort.

Frequently people rush ahead of God and start businesses or ministries, and then, when their bills are not being paid and their responsibilities are not being met, they expect others to bail them out. Many of them say, "I am living by faith." But that gives faith a bad name. If they were truly living by faith, their families would be fed and clothed. Too many launch out on presumption or foolishness, without clear guidance from God. How can they expect God to supply all their needs?

THE TIMING OF GOD'S PROVISION

God expects us to be faithful to provide for our families, just as He is faithful to provide for His. If our children are suffering because of some decision we have made then the Scriptures are clear: we are worse than unbelievers. It doesn't matter how spiritual we may appear. We must be more careful to get God's leading in these matters if we expect Him to pay the bills for us.

When our families suffer, they lose respect for us and for God. This ought not to be, beloved.

Many years ago, the Lord pulled me out of full-time ministry for a time. I knew that I was called to be in full-time ministry eventually, but, for the time being, I got a job to support my wife and children. My first job, thanks to the graciousness of friends, was to clean a McDonald's restaurant at night. I scraped up gum, wiped up broken eggs from the cooking area and cleaned the toilets. All the while, I prayed that the restaurant would cook too much food so that I could take home some leftover hamburgers to my family.

As I learned to be responsible, I was promoted. Then I got a better job. When yet another job came open and the salary was double what I was making, I was sure it was the right thing to do. And it seemed assured. The interview was just a formality I was told. I was so excited ... until the Lord told me not to take the job, to stay where I was for the time being.

I was perplexed. Why would I not accept a job that doubled my salary? Each day, as I drove back and forth to work, I pondered this matter. I became aware of a new building going up and my interest was drawn to it many times. After some months, one morning I saw a sign put up on the building which said: "Grand Opening." I called that same morning and asked about a job.

The business was to be open twenty-four hours a day, I was told, and they needed crews around the clock. Did they have any more openings? They still needed a night auditor, but they were bringing someone from Honolulu because the work involved a rather new machine. They thought it would be the first of its kind in Maui and had been told that it required time to learn to use it well. "We need to bring in someone who already knows that machine," the gentleman told me, "even though we will have to pay for their moving expenses."

"What kind of machine is it?" I asked.

"A Micros," he answered.

The Provision of God

In that moment I was elated and understood why the Lord had not allowed me to change jobs. For the past two years I had been using that very machine, and I knew that this company would now hire me. That is exactly what happened, and I was with that fine firm until God put me back into full-time ministry.

LIVING IN LO DEBAR

God's provision for us is so wonderful. He has so much planned for us, and He will enable us to carry it out. Why, then, are so many believers still living in Lo Debar?

> *Now David said, "Is there still anyone who is left of the house of Saul, that I may show him kindness for Jonathan's sake?" And there was a servant of the house of Saul whose name was Ziba. So when they had called him to David, the king said to him, "Are you Ziba?"*
> *And he said, "At your service!"*
> *Then the king said, "Is there not still someone of the house of Saul, to whom I may show the kindness of God?"*
> *And Ziba said to the king, "There is still a son of Jonathan who is lame in his feet."*
> *So the king said to him, "Where is he?"*
> *And Ziba said to the king, "Indeed he is in the house of Machir the son of Ammiel, in Lo Debar."*
> 2 Samuel 9:1-4

Lo Debar means "a place of no pasture." There was

no provision in that place. It was the dwelling place of Jonathan's son, Mephibosheth, and because of the covenant David had made with his friend Jonathan, Mephibosheth had a right to the king's palace and to the king's provision. Despite this fact, he was still dwelling in Lo Debar, the place of no pasture, the place of no provision.

How many of God's covenant children are dwelling in Lo Debar today? Far too many, and it doesn't have to be so. Each of us should be dwelling in the place of God's glorious provision, eating at His table. God has given us a Covenant and it is time for us to receive its provisions. This happened for Jonathan's son:

> *So Mephibosheth dwelt in Jerusalem, for he ate continually at the king's table. And he was lame in both his feet.* 2 Samuel 9:13

If you are living in Lo Debar, not experiencing God's provision in your life, then know that God wants you to come out of that place of leanness today and into Jerusalem — the place of peace and plenty.

OUR OWN WORST ENEMY

Sometimes, when our needs are not supplied, we may find that we are our own worst enemy and that we are unwittingly robbing ourselves:

> *"For I am the* LORD, *I do not change;*
> *Therefore you are not consumed, O sons of Jacob.*
> *Yet from the days of your fathers*

The Provision of God

You have gone away from My ordinances
And have not kept them.
Return to Me, and I will return to you,"
Says the LORD of hosts.
"But you said, 'In what way shall we return?'
Will a man rob God?
Yet you have robbed Me!
But you say,
'In what way have we robbed You?'
In tithes and offerings.
You are cursed with a curse,
For you have robbed Me,
Even this whole nation.
Bring all the tithes into the storehouse,
That there may be food in My house,
And try Me now in this,"
Says the LORD of hosts,
"If I will not open for you the windows of heaven
And pour out for you such blessing
That there will not be room enough to receive it."

Malachi 3:6-10

"I am the Lord. I change not." God does not change. He is *"the same yesterday, today, and forever"* (Hebrews 13:8). If He was the Provider in the Old Testament, if He was the Provider in the Gospels, if He was the Provider in the Epistles, then He is still the Provider today. If we have no provision, therefore, it may be our fault, not God's.

In the time of the prophet Malachi, Israel had turned from God, and it was that turning that had produced their woes. God promised them that if they would return to Him, His provision would return to them. It's just that simple.

When we speak of provision as a means of guidance, therefore, we must understand that this is only valid in the lives of obedient Christians. God will not affirm disobedience. If you are robbing God, if you're not seeking Him, He will not confirm what you are doing by prospering you or your acts. Don't expect such confirmation, for it will never come. Expecting God to supply your needs assumes that you are consciously doing His will. Otherwise, it just won't work.

Provision was guaranteed to the people of Israel only as long as they followed the Lord and His will for their lives. They were not to look for His provision unless they were willing to put Him first.

One of the ways God tested the obedience of the Israelites was to require that they bring their tithes into the storehouse. This, for us today, represents the local church where we are fed. Tithes are the first-fruits of our labor and our increase, and God is not satisfied when we bring Him just leftovers — after all our bills have been paid. Giving our first-fruits demonstrates to God that we recognize Him as the Source of all our blessing and that we are willing to honor Him with our increase.

If we are following after God with all that we have, and we are honoring Him with our tithes, finances should never be our primary problem. When we are faithful to *"prove the Lord,"* He gives us a wonderful promise:

> *"And I will rebuke the devourer for your sakes,*
> *So that he will not destroy the fruit of your ground,*

The Provision of God

Nor shall the vine fail to bear fruit for you in the field,"
Says the LORD *of hosts;*
"And all nations will call you blessed,
For you will be a delightful land,"
Says the LORD *of hosts.*   Malachi 3:11-12

If we are not obeying God, we cannot rebuke the devourer, and neither can we get God to rebuke the devourer for us. Furthermore, it will not do us any good to pray and believe for His provision when this is the case. Instead of an open Heaven for blessing, we have created an open door to bondage, and if we want to close that door, we must learn to put the Lord first. That includes the area of finances.

God will guide us throughout our life in Him, if we will allow Him to do so. All of His principles work together to help God's children to see His plan. Learn how to use each of the seven in your life: the inner conviction of the Spirit, the Holy Scriptures, prophecy, godly counsel, circumstances, the peace of God, and the provision of God. Let these principles of *God's Guidance System* work together in your life so that you can hear and heed the voice of the Lord.

Part III:

The Application

CHAPTER 10

APPLYING THESE TRUTHS TO YOUR LIFE

For whom He foreknew, He also predestined to be conformed to the image of His Son, that He might be the firstborn among many brethren. Moreover whom He predestined, these He also called; whom He called, these He also justified; and whom He justified, these He also glorified. What then shall we say to these things? If God is for us, who can be against us?

Romans 8:29-31

There is a lot of pain in the Church today which, unfortunately, could be avoided. There are losses of revenue, broken relationships, inner hurts and terrible tragedy in many lives. Why should this state exist in the Church of the Lord Jesus Christ? Often, it is simply because we have not understood *God's Guidance System* well enough, for how can we respond to the guidance of the Lord if we do not recognize it when it operates in our lives?

God's Guidance System

I have noticed that most mistakes occur in the lives of Christians, young and old alike, when anyone places too much emphasis on only one principle of guidance to the exclusion of the others. This is an unscriptural position to take, but many do it through a lack of understanding.

For example, someone says, "Three people called me to confirm this." While it is true that they might have received three phone calls from three different people and all three individuals said the same thing, at the same time there may be other signals God is using to tell them otherwise. Because they are fixated on the three people who agree, however, they can't hear what God is saying.

WE HEAR WHAT WE WANT TO HEAR

Sometimes we hear what we want to hear. My experience as a pastor has shown me that generally those who only look to one means of guidance do so because they find someone who agrees with them and they want to have their own way. They use what they think they know or are familiar with to confirm what they want to do. These people realize that if they ask for counsel, or if they receive a personal prophetic word, or if they look to any other means of guidance, the answer will surely be negative. So they avoid it.

None of us wants to hear "no," for by nature we want what we want, and we want it when we want it. This is also a symptom of our age. Children today don't want to be denied anything, and when they grow to adulthood, they will still not want to be denied anything — even by God. When this is true, we look for ways around

Applying These Truths to YOUR Life

what we know to be clear guidance from the Lord, so we can get what we want, and this is dangerous.

The results of all this are a lot of wrong decisions, a lot of anger about why things are not working out well for us, and a lot of frustration with those around us and the situations we happen to find ourselves in. It is time to learn a better way.

FROM THIS MOMENT FORTH

Every major decision you make, from this moment forth, should be made on the strength of at least two, and preferably three or more witnesses, or principles of God's guidance. The greater the decision, the more witnesses you will need — if you want to be confident that you have always made the very best decision.

That doesn't mean we will always like what God tells us. There have been times when I have received counsel — from my pastors or from the eldership or from my wife — that I was not ready to hear. It would have been much easier to just run ahead of what God was showing me through that counsel. At least, it might have been easier at first. I have learned, however, that I cannot violate these principles and not expect to eventually pay the consequences.

Jesus said:

I am the way, the truth, and the life. No one comes to the Father except through Me. John 14:6

He did not say, "I am a way, I am a truth, I am a life." He is *the* way and *the* truth and *the* life, and if we know

what's good for us we will seek to know His ways better and seek to follow them as carefully as possible. It is
foolish to do otherwise.

In God, we have a great future. He cares for us and
wants us to succeed. He has a wonderful plan for each
of our lives.

Every child of God can rest in the assurance that He
is on our side, that He is fighting for our welfare. It is
because of this that we can depend on His plans and
rest in the knowledge that His will is always best for us.
He knows so much better than we do what tomorrow
holds and what we need to do to prosper.

THE POOR TESTIMONIES OF SOME

The "testimony" of some Christians has frightened
away many who were considering giving their lives to
Christ, for these "testimonies" sound more like horror
stories. "After I came to the Lord, I lost my business and
then my home. Then my wife left me. After that my dog
died ..." And they go on and on like this. Thank God for
people who have gone through terrible times and can
testify of God's goodness and faithfulness to deliver and
redeem, but the world deserves to hear better testimonies than these. They need to hear that the Christian life
works, that it bears fruit, that it brings blessing. If Christians are a total disaster, what message does that convey
to the world?

You owe it to yourself and to others not to wander
around any longer in darkness, just hoping you are making the right choices, praying that you are doing the right
thing. God has provided tried and true methods to pre-

vent you from making mistakes. He wants to lead you *"into green pastures"* and *"beside still waters."* He wants you to finish your course without having the constant ups and downs that many experience and without making a shipwreck of your life and the lives of others.

We all make mistakes, and until we reach the presence of the Lord, we will probably continue to make mistakes. Those mistakes, however, need not be the fatal type that take so many out of the race and send them on their way back into darkness and despair. When we make a mistake, we must recognize it, repent of it, and get back on track so that we can continue on course for eternity with God.

Our God is not out to punish us or put us down. He does, however, expect us to repent where repentance is called for, and He does expect us to change our ways where change is needed. But all this is so that we can be free of the sin that the writer of the Hebrews said *"so easily ensnares,"* and so that we can be free to *"run with endurance the race that is set before us"* (Hebrews 12:1).

It is time to stop playing hide-and-seek with God. Each of us must be able to discern His will for our individual lives. We must know where we are going and what to expect when we get there. None of us should be walking around blind. The result of that is to wind up in a ditch somewhere, waiting for someone to come along and pull us out. Let God take off your blinders so that you can know what the Spirit of the Lord is saying.

"HE WHO HAS EARS"

The problem is not with God. He is speaking just as clearly and just as precisely today as He did in the days of the biblical prophets. Just as He inspired men to write the Bible, He desires to give each of us detailed instructions concerning life. But are we listening? Jesus' continual cry while He was on Earth was:

He who has ears to hear, let him hear!
Matthew 11:15

And that is still the cry of the heart of God today. When John received his great revelation on the Isle of Patmos concerning the church in various ages and even in this day in which we live, he heard the Spirit saying about the church then and now:

He who has an ear, let him hear what the Spirit says to the churches.
Revelation 2:7, 11, 17, 29, 3:6, 13 and 22

This is a life and death matter. We can no longer afford to be turning left when God is turning right. Turning left may make more sense to us, but God knows the final outcome. The only place of safety is by His side, wherever He happens to be at the moment.

We live in an amazing age, when scientists have filled the heavens with satellites of every description. This has been successfully accomplished only because the science of guidance has progressed to the place that not only can each satellite be launched successfully into a unique orbit, but it can be held in that orbit so that it does not interfere with thousands of other objects in space. Think about it! The world has gotten far ahead of us on this matter of guidance.

Applying These Truths to YOUR Life

Scientists, however, have learned the hard way. By losing expensive satellites during launch and during orbit, they have learned that a slight error in the adjustment of the guidance systems of either the launch rocket or the thrusters that keep satellites in place can mean sure disaster.

Get your instruments tuned up. We have a great journey to make and we don't want anything to hinder us along the way.

Stop blaming God. He is never vague about the directions He gives. He has set us in secure paths, paths of blessing and prosperity, paths that will lead us eventually into eternal life in His presence. When you mess up and get off course, don't try to place the blame on Him. He is not a God of confusion. And stop blaming your fellow believers for your wobbly orbit. The course has been laid out straight before you. Get on it.

This is not a guessing game. You are not on an eternal scavenger hunt. Life is not a puzzle to play with. God is serious about this matter, and it is time for us to get serious about it too.

GOD IN THE INFORMATION AGE

Every major decision in life requires knowledge — knowledge of the facts involved, knowledge of the people involved, and knowledge of the circumstances. We cannot possibly know all these things by ourselves. We need God more than ever before.

The Proverbs declare:

Through wisdom a house is built, And by understand-

ing it is established; By knowledge the rooms are filled with all precious and pleasant riches.

Proverbs 24:3-4

Stop gambling with your future. Move out of your comfort zone and start learning to hear from God. Stop doing what is convenient at the moment and start doing what will reap eternal rewards. Anyone can coast through life, but when you do that you might just coast right into a wall. Start moving against the current. You can move mountains and effect change in your world.

God's plan for your life is unique, and only you can fulfill it. I can't tell you what it is; only God can. I do know that He wants you to prosper and have success. He is committed to your prosperity and will give you the strength, the wisdom and the resources to achieve it — as you are willing to follow Him. What could be more wonderful!

The devil would be delighted if you just continue to stumble through life without finding proper guidance. He loves it when you find yourself in some ditch, bogged down, unable to move and unable to accomplish anything of importance. God wants to get you out of that ditch and make you an overcomer. He wants you to finish well — with your marriage, your children, your business, your ministry and, above all, with your relationship with Him. The choice is yours.

Inner conviction or what we commonly call hearing the voice of God, the extensive truths of the Scriptures, prophetic utterance, godly counsel, circumstances, the peace of God and the provision of God: all these have been given to us to shed light along our pathway and to

Applying These Truths to YOUR Life

bring us safely through life's journey. The God of the Universe is ready to be your official Guide through life, if you only accord Him the privilege. Let all of His principles of guidance work together to help you see more clearly His plan for your tomorrows.

Amen!

For as many as are led by the Spirit of God, these are sons of God.

Romans 8:14

Ministry address:

Dr. Les Brown
Higher Ground Ministries
P.O. Box 4113
Kahului, HI 96733
E-mail: 104767.3455@compuserve.com